MISTER
ROBERTS

MISTER ROBERTS

ROBERTS

BY
THOMAS
HEGGEN

ILLUSTRATED BY SAMUEL HANKS BRYANT

HOUGHTON MIFFLIN COMPANY BOSTON

TWENTY-SECOND PRINTING   C

ISBN: 0-395-07788-5

Acknowledgment is made to *Atlantic
Monthly* magazine for their permission to use some of the stories in this
volume.

PRINTED IN THE U.S.A.

FOR

CAROL LYNN

INTRODUCTION

Now, IN THE WANING DAYS of the second World War, this ship lies at anchor in the glassy bay of one of the back islands of the Pacific. It is a Navy cargo ship. You know it as a cargo ship by the five yawning hatches, by the house amidships, by the booms that bristle from the masts like mechanical arms. You know it as a Navy ship by the color (dark, dull blue), by the white numbers painted on the bow, and unfailingly by the thin ribbon of the commission pennant flying from the mainmast. In the Navy Register, this ship is listed as the *Reluctant*. Its crew never refer to it by name: to them it is always 'this bucket.'

In an approximate way it is possible to fix this ship in time. The local civil time is 0614 and the day is one in the spring of 1945. Sunrise was three minutes ago and the officer-of-the-deck is not quite alert, for the red truck lights atop the masts are still burning. It is a breathless time, quiet and fresh and lovely. The water inside the bay is planed to perfect smoothness, and in the emergent light it is bronze-colored, and not yet blue. The sky, which will be an intense blue, is also dulled a little by the film of night. The inflamed sun floats an inch or so above the horizon, and the wine-red light it spreads does not hurt the eyes at all. Over on the island there begin to be signs of life. An arm of blue smoke climbs straight and clean from the palm groves. Down on the dock people are moving about. A jeep goes by on the beach road and leaves a puff of dust behind. But on this ship there seems to be no one stirring. Just off the bow, a school of flying fish breaks the water suddenly. In the quiet the effect is as startling as an explosion.

In Germany right now it would be seven o'clock at night. It would be quite dark, and perhaps there is a cold rain falling. In this darkness and in this rain the Allied armies are slogging on toward Berlin. Some stand as close as one hundred and fifty miles. Aachen and Cologne have fallen, inside of days Hanover will fall. Far around the girdle of the world, at Okinawa Gunto it is now three in the morning. Flares would be dripping their slow, wet light as the United States Tenth Army finishes its job. These are contemporary moments of that in which our ship lies stagnant in the bay.

Surely, then, since this is One World, the tranquil ship is only an appearance, this somnolence an illusion. Surely an artillery shell fired at Hanover ripples the air here. Surely a bomb dopped on Okinawa trembles these bulkheads. This is an American Man o' War, manned by American Fighting Men: who would know

better than they that this is One World? Who indeed?
Of course, then, this indolence is only seeming, this
lethargy a façade: in actuality this ship must be throb-
bing with grim purposefulness, intense activity, and a
high awareness of its destiny. Of course.

Let us go aboard this Man o' War.

Step carefully there over little Red McLaughlin,
sleeping on the hatch cover. Red is remarkable for
being able to sleep anywhere: probably he was on his
way down to the compartment when he dropped in his
tracks, sound asleep. There do not, in truth, seem to be
many people up yet — but then it is still a few minutes to
reveille. Reveille is at six-thirty. In the Chief's quarters there is one man up: it is Johnson, the chief master-
at-arms. He is the one who makes reveille. Johnson is
drinking coffee and he seems preoccupied: perhaps, as
you suggest, his mind is thousands of miles away, following the battle-line in Germany. But no — to tell the
truth — it is not. Johnson is thinking of a can of beer,
and he is angry. Last night he hid the can carefully
beneath a pile of dirty scivvies in his locker: now it is
gone. Johnson is reasonably certain that Yarby, the
chief yeoman, took it; but he cannot prove this. He is
turning over in his mind ways of getting back at Yarby.
Let us move on.

Down in the armory a group of six men sits tensely
around a wooden box. You say they are discussing forti-
fications? — you distinctly heard the word 'sandbag'
spoken? Yes, you did: but it is feared that you heard it
out of context. What Olson, the first-class gunner's

mate, said was: 'Now watch the son-of-a-bitch sandbag me!' Used like that, it is a common colloquialism of poker: this is an all-night poker game.

We find our way now to the crew's compartment. You are surprised to see so many men sleeping, and so soundly? Perhaps it would be revelatory to peer into their dreams. No doubt, as you say, we will find them haunted by battles fought and battles imminent. This man who snores so noisily is Stefanowski, machinist's mate second class. His dream? . . . well . . . there is a girl . . . she is inadequately clothed . . . she is smiling at Stefanowski . . . let us not intrude.

You are doubtless right: certainly an officer will be more sensitive. In this stateroom, with his hand dangling over the side of the bunk, is Ensign Pulver. He is one of the engineering officers. And you *are* right; his dream *is* conditioned by the war. In his dream he is all alone in a lifeboat. He is lying there on a leather couch and there are cases of Schlitz beer stacked all about him. On the horizon he sees the ship go down at last; it goes down slowly, stern first. A swimming figure reaches the boat and clutches the gunwales. Without rising from his couch, Ensign Pulver takes the ball-bat at his side and smashes the man's hands. Every time the man gets his hands on the gunwales, Pulver pounds them with the bat. Finally the man sinks in a froth of bubbles. Who is this man — a Jap? No, it is the Captain. Ensign Pulver smiles happily and opens a can of beer.

What manner of ship is this? What does it do? What

is its combat record? Well, those are fair questions, if
difficult ones. The *Reluctant,* as was said, is a naval
auxiliary. It operates in the back areas of the Pacific.
In its holds it carries food and trucks and dungarees
and toothpaste and toilet paper. For the most part it
stays on its regular run, from Tedium to Apathy and
back; about five days each way. It makes an occasional
trip to Monotony, and once it made a run all the way
to Ennui, a distance of two thousand nautical miles
from Tedium. It performs its dreary and unthanked
job, and performs it, if not inspiredly, then at least
adequately.

It has shot down no enemy planes, nor has it fired
upon any, nor has it seen any. It has sunk with its guns
no enemy subs, but there *was* this once that it fired.
This periscope, the lookout sighted it way off on the
port beam, and the Captain, who was scared almost out
of his mind, gave the order: 'Commence firing!' The
five-inch and the two port three-inch guns fired for perhaps ten minutes, and the showing was really rather
embarrassing. The closest shell was three hundred
yards off, and all the time the unimpressed periscope
stayed right there. At one thousand yards it was identi-
fied as the protruding branch of a floating tree. The
branch had a big bend in it and didn't even look much
like a periscope.

So now you know: that is the kind of ship the *Reluctant* is. Admittedly it is not an heroic ship. Whether,
though, you can also denounce its men as unheroic is
another matter. Before that is summarily done, a few

obvious facts about heroism should perhaps be pleaded; the first of them being that there are *kinds* of it. On this ship, for instance, you might want to consider Lieutenant Roberts as a hero. Lieutenant Roberts is a young man of sensitivity, perceptiveness, and idealism; attributes which are worthless and even inimical to such a community as this. He wants to be in the war; he is powerfully drawn to the war and to the general desolation of the time, but he is held off, frustrated, defeated by the rather magnificently non-conductive character of his station. He is the high-strung instrument assuming the low-strung rôle. He has geared himself to the tempo of the ship and made the adjustment with — the words are not believed misplaced — gallantry, courage, and fortitude. Perhaps he is a kind of hero.

And then in simple justice to the undecorated men of the *Reluctant* it should also be pointed out that heroism — physical heroism — is very much a matter of opportunity. On the physical level heroism is not so much an act, implying volition, as it is a reflex. Apply the rubber hammer to the patella tendon and, commonly, you produce the knee jerk. Apply the situation permitting bravery to one hundred young males with actively functioning adrenal glands and, reasonably, you would produce seventy-five instances of clear-cut heroism. Would, that is, but for one thing: that after the fifty-first the word would dissolve into meaninglessness. Like the knee jerk, physical courage is perhaps latent and even implicit in the individual, needing only the application of situation, of opportunity, to reveal it. A case in point: Ensign Pulver.

Ensign Pulver is a healthy, highly normal young man who sleeps a great deal, is amiable, well-liked, and generally regarded by his shipmates as being rather worthless. At the instigation of forces well beyond his control, he joined the Naval Reserve and by the same forces was assigned to this ship, where he spends his time sleeping, discoursing, and plotting ingenious offensives against the Captain which he never executes. Alter the accidents, apply the situation, locate Pulver in the ball turret of a B-29 over Japan, and what do you have? You have Pulver, the Congressional Medal man, who single-handedly and successively shot down twenty-three attacking Zekes, fought the fire raging in his own ship, with his bare hands held together the severed wing struts and with his bare feet successfully landed the grievously wounded plane on its home field.

These, then — if the point is taken — are unheroic men only because they are non-combatant; whether unwillingly or merely unavoidably is not important. They fight no battles: *ergo* in a certain literal and narrow sense they are non-combatant. But in the larger vision these men are very definitely embattled, and rather curiously so. The enemy is not the unseen Jap, not the German, nor the abstract villainy of fascism: it is that credible and tangible villain, the Captain. The warfare is declared and continual, and the lines have long been drawn. On one side is the Captain, alone; opposing him are the other one hundred and seventy-eight members, officers and men, of the ship's company. It is quite an even match.

The Captain of a naval vessel is a curious affair. Personally he may be short, scrawny, unprepossessing; but a Captain is not a person and cannot be viewed as such. He is an embodiment. He is given stature, substance, and sometimes a new dimension by the massive, cumulative authority of the Navy Department which looms behind him like a shadow. With some Captains this shadow is a great, terrifying cloud; with others, it is scarcely apparent at all: but with none can it go unnoticed. Now to this the necessary exception: Captain Morton. With Captain Morton it could and does up to a point go unnoticed. The crew knows instinctively that the Captain is vulnerable, that he is unaware of the full dimensions of his authority; and, thus stripped of his substance, they find him detestable and not at all terrifying. He is not hated, for in hate there is something of fear and something of respect, neither of which is present here. And you could not say loathed, for loathing is passive and this is an active feeling. Best say detested; vigorously disliked. As the chosen enemy he is the object of an incessant guerrilla warfare, which is, for the Navy, a most irregular business. Flat declarations like 'Captain Morton is an old fart' appear in chalk from time to time on gun mounts; cigarette butts, an obsession of the Captain's, are mysteriously inserted into his cabin; his telephone rings at odd hours of the night; once when he was standing on the quarterdeck a helmet dropped from the flying bridge missed him by perhaps a yard — the margin of a warning. Childishness? Pettiness? Perhaps: but remember that these

are the only weapons the men have. Remember that
they are really hopelessly outmatched. Remember that
the shadow, acknowledged or not, is there all the time.

Captain Morton is a tall bulging middle-aged man
with a weak chin and a ragged mustache. He is bow-
legged and broad-beamed (for which the crew would
substitute 'lard-assed'), and he walks with the absurd
roll of an animated Popeye. If you ask, any crew member will give you the bill of particulars against the Captain, but he will be surprised that you find it necessary
to ask. He will tell you that the man is stupid, incompetent, petty, vicious, treacherous. The signalmen or
yeomen will insist that he is unable to understand the
simplest message or letter. Anyone in the deck divisions
will tell you that he is far more concerned with keeping
the decks cleared of cigarette butts than with discharging cargo, his nominal mission. All of the crew will tell
you of the petty persecution he directs against them:
the preposterous insistence (for an auxiliary operating
in the rear areas) that men topside wear hats and shirts
at all times; the shouting and grumbling and name-
calling; the stubborn refusal to permit recreation parties
ashore; the absurd and constantly increasing prohibi-
tions against leaning on the rail, sleeping on deck, gum-
chewing, heavy-soled shoes, that and this and that.
And you will be told with damning finality that the
man is vulgar, foul-mouthed. In an indelicate community this charge may appear surprising, but of all it
is clearly the most strongly laid.

These are the ostensible reasons for the feeling

against the Captain; and possibly, possibly not, they are the real ones. It is for a student of causative psychology to determine whether the Captain created his own situation, or whether it was born, sired by boredom and dammed by apathy, of the need for such an obsessional pastime. The only thing abundantly certain is that it is there.

Now on this slumbrous ship, this battle-ground, this bucket, there is sudden movement. Chief Johnson leans back in his chair, yawns, stretches, and gets up. He looks at his watch — 0629 — time to make reveille. He picks up his whistle, yawns again, and shuffles forward to the crew's compartment. Now there will be action on this torpid ship. Now the day will spring to life; now men will swarm the decks and the sounds of purposeful activity fill the air. Now at least, at reveille, this Man o' War will look the part.

Chief Johnson blows his whistle fiercely in the compartment. He starts forward and works aft among the bunks croaking in a raw, sing-song voice: 'Reveille . . . Hit the deck! . . . Rise and shine! . . . Get out of them goddamn sacks! . . . What the hell you trying to do, sleep your life away? . . . Reveille . . . Hit the deck! . . .' He is like a raucous minstrel, the way he chants and wanders through the compartment. Here and there an eye cocks open and looks tolerantly upon the Chief; now and then a forgiving voice mumbles sleepily, 'Okay chief okay . . .' but not a body moves, not a muscle stirs.

Chief Johnson reaches the after door. He turns

around for a moment and surveys the sagging bunks. He has done his job: he has observed the rules. Some of these men, he knows, will get up in half an hour to eat breakfast. Most of the rest, the ones who don't eat breakfast, will probably get up at eight. Chief Johnson walks sleepily aft and turns in his own bunk to sleep until eight. Eight c'clock is a reasonable hour for a man's arising; and this is, above all else, a reasonable ship.

T HERE WERE FOURTEEN OFFICERS on the *Reluctant*
and all of them were Reserves. Captain Morton was a
lieutenant-commander, and on the outside had been in
the merchant marine, where he claimed to hold a
master's license. Mr. LeSueur, the executive officer,

1

also a lieutenant-commander and also ex-merchant marine, swore that the Captain held only a first mate's license. Mr. LeSueur was a capable man who kept to himself and raged against the Captain with a fine singleness of purpose. The other officers represented the miscellany of pre-war America. Ensign Keith and Ensign Moulton had been college boys. Lieutenant (jg) Ed Pauley had been an insurance salesman. Lieutenant Carney had been a shoe clerk. Lieutenant (jg) Langston had been a school-teacher. The new mantle of leadership fell uneasily upon these officers. Most of them, feeling ridiculous in it, renounced the rôle altogether and behaved as if they had no authority and no responsibility. Excepting Mr. LeSueur, excepting categorically the Captain, and excepting the Doctor as a special case, there was only one of these Reserves who successfully impersonated an officer, and he least of all was trying to. That was Lieutenant Roberts. He was a born leader; there is no other kind.

Lieutenant Roberts was the First Lieutenant of the *Reluctant.* The First Lieutenant of a ship is charged with its maintenance; he bosses the endless round of cleaning, scraping, painting, and repairing necessary to its upkeep. In itself the job is a considerable one and in this case the only real one on the ship but Roberts had yet another job: cargo officer. That was one hell of a job. Roberts was out on deck all the time that the ship was working cargo, and whenever there was a special hurry about loading or discharging, he could figure on three days without sleep. And all the time he was standing deck watches, one in four, day in and out. He got very little sleep. He was a slender, blond boy of twenty-six and he had a shy, tilted smile. He was rather quiet, and his voice was soft and flat, but there was something in it that made people strain to listen. When he was angry he was very formidable, for without raising his voice he could achieve a savage, lashing sarcasm. He had been a medical student on the outside; he loathed the Captain; and all the circumstances of his present station were an agony to him. The crew worshiped him.

They really did. Devotion of a sort can be bought or commanded or bullied or begged, but it was accorded Roberts unanimously and voluntarily. He was the sort of leader who is followed blindly because he does not look back to see if he is being followed. For him the crew would turn out ten times the work that any other officer on the ship could command. He could not pass the galley without being offered a steak sandwich, or the bakery without a pie. At one time or another perhaps ninety per cent of the crew had asked him for advice. If it had been said of him once in the compartment it had been said a hundred times: 'The best son-of-a-bitching officer in the goddamn Navy.'

The officers, who lived with Roberts as equals and could therefore judge him less emotionally, felt much the same way. Being less interdependent than the crew, the officers were correspondingly less unified, and were split into at least four definite and mutually exclusive groups. Roberts, although he allied himself with none of these cliques, was *ex officio* a member of all, and was sought by all. It was unthinkable that Ed Pauley enter the stateroom of Carney and Lieutenant (jg) Billings, and vice versa. The Doctor's room was forever closed to Ensign Moulton, end vice versa. Langston could sooner pass through a needle's eye than the doorway to the room of Lieutenant (jg) Gonaud, the supply officer. All of these doors were enthusiastically open to Roberts, and to no other officer. His special friends were Ed Pauley, who had to offer an easy sociability; the Doc, who offered that plus intellectual comradeship; and Ensign Pulver, whose contribution was hard to define. Ensign Pulver thought that Roberts was approximately God, and admired equally and uncritically everything that he did. He was almost shameless in the way, literally and figuratively, that he dogged Roberts's footsteps. Without ever inviting one or desiring one, Roberts had acquired a disciple.

The only enemy Roberts had was the Captain, who hated his guts. Ed Pauley kept in his room a small chart that listed all of the officers and after their names varying numbers of blue and red crosses. A blue cross represented a direct threat or insult from the Captain, and counted two red crosses. A red cross stood for an insult or slander from the Captain delivered secondhand to someone else. And on this chart Roberts's name led all the rest, even though his record consisted almost entirely of the red crosses representing hand-me-down calumny. The Captain had a noticeable reticence about upbraiding Roberts to his face.

That would be one obvious reason for the Captain's hostility toward Roberts; he was afraid of him. He had no hold over Roberts and he knew it. If Roberts had asked once for a transfer, he had asked twenty times, and every time the Captain had turned him down. The Captain had done that out of spite, of course, but also from a sensible awareness of Roberts's value to the ship. Roberts was irrefutably competent and the Captain hated him for that, too; for Captain Morton was irrefutably and unbelievably incompetent. On two different occasions Lieutenant Roberts had saved the ship in convoy from fairly imminent collisions invited by the Captain's inept conning. The Captain felt no demonstrable gratitude. He repaid Roberts in the only coin he knew: by haranguing him over trifling details, by calling him names *in absentia,* and by keeping him aboard the ship. The petty and sneaking abuse merely amused Roberts, but the prison of the ship was an endless torture to him and a mounting despair beyond which, finally, he couldn't see.

He had been aboard the *Reluctant* two and one-half years, longer than any other officer. He alone on the ship sincerely wanted to fight the war, and he worked cargo and kept the ship painted and stood watches. He alone sincerely hated the ship, and it lay unbidden in the palm of his hand. He *had* to get into the war, but in a chaos that blandly reduced imperative to impossible he ran up and down the dreary islands of the back areas. He tried very hard not to let himself get disorganized, and for the most part he succeeded simply by reading a great deal, by talking with his friends, and by working until sleep was unavoidable. Sometimes, though, the pressure inside him became too strong, and then he prowled the ship with an uncontrollable restlessness.

On one such evening Lieutenant Roberts left the movie early. The movies were the great opiate of the ship. They were held every night in port, and everyone attended except the men on watch, and many of them attended too. The screen was rigged on the mast-table forward of number three hatch and the crew sat on the hatch cover and on boxes and a few chairs on the deck. The officers sat regally in chairs on the quarterdeck, the Captain in the center. There was only one projector so that at the end of every reel there was a pause while the new reel was wound on. This was always a noisy period, with much shouting back and forth, much speculation on the heroine's chastity, and many offers to share her bed. The movies were the one great social function of the ship. No matter how bad they were — and they were consistently bad and always ancient — everyone but Roberts stayed grimly to the end. Roberts could seldom stomach them beyond the fourth reel.

Tonight, because he was restless and because the movie was a surpassingly stupid Western, he quit after the first reel. For a while he walked up and down in the area just abaft the house. Then he went up to the flying bridge and stood for a while looking out over the bay. Then he went down to the wardroom. Out of old habit he looked into the refrigerator in the pantry, found a few olives and ate them. He poured a cup of coffee and drank it. Then he drifted along the passageway looking into each stateroom for someone to talk with. There was no one. Finally he went into Ensign Pulver's room.

Pulver lived alone in a double room. He slept in the bottom bunk and used the top one as a general file for everything that couldn't decently be strewn on the deck. It now contained a soiled scivvy shirt, a pair of soiled khaki trousers, an orange, half a dozen books, a thick pile of old magazines, and the harmonica with which Pulver achieved an eerie caterwauling effect on the only two tunes that he knew. Roberts looked now at the books. One of them was *Nana* which Pulver was currently reading in an English translation. Then he examined the magazine file. Pulver had a well-known faculty for attracting all the loose magazines on the ship. Roberts found a year-old *Cosmopolitan* that he hadn't seen, and he stretched out in Pulver's bunk and started looking through it.

He hadn't been there long when there were shuffling footsteps and Ensign Pulver came in. Roberts looked up, surprised. He didn't know anything short of leg chains that could keep Pulver from a movie.

'What's the matter with you?' he said. 'You sick?'

Pulver flopped dejectedly in the chair and locked his hands behind his head. 'Hell,' he said, 'what a stinking movie!'

'Since when did you object to stinking movies?' Roberts asked.

Pulver looked faintly hurt. 'Hell,' he said, 'I like a

good picture all right, but not one like this. Besides,' he added, 'that miserable bastard had a chance to get a really good movie tonight and he took this one instead.'

'Who's that?'

'The old man. This ship astern of us wanted to trade us *Since You Went Away* — that's almost brand-new — and he took this damn shoot-em-up!'

Roberts folded the magazine across his stomach. 'Well,' he said, 'that's not surprising.'

Pulver said disgustedly: 'And he's sitting up there now chortling and having a big time!'

'That's to be expected,' Roberts said. 'He's found his own level of entertainment.'

Ensign Pulver shook his head gloomily. 'Did you hear what he did today?' he asked suddenly.

'Probably,' Roberts said. 'What did he do?'

'He was prowling around the rooms this afternoon and he caught five officers in their sacks. Now ——'

Roberts interrupted: 'Needless to say you were one of them.'

'Yeah,' said Pulver, 'I was one. Now he's putting out a new order that says all officers will stay out of their sacks during working hours. He told the exec that if they don't he's going to have all the mattresses removed during the day and he's going to take down all the doors so he can walk around and see who's in bed. Jesus,' said Pulver, 'did you ever hear of such a simple bastard?'

Roberts smiled. 'He's certainly simple if he thinks he's going to keep you out of your sack.'

He had touched upon a sore spot. Although he con-
scientiously spent better than two-thirds of each day
in his bunk, Ensign Pulver always got aggrieved when
charged with this. His argument was that he actually
slept very little, and that most of his time in bed he
was thinking. He answered now a little stiffly, 'I'm not
in there as much as you think. I'm not in there half as
much as Billings!'

Roberts was not disposed to be charitable. 'Maybe
not' — he conceded nothing. 'It's true that you do get
up for meals once in a while!'

'Hell,' said Pulver defensively. He sniffed, rubbed
his nose, and minutely examined his fingernails. Then
he thought to change the subject.

'What the hell's the matter with that stupid bastard
anyhow?' he asked.

'Which one is that?'

'The Old Man. What's really the matter with him
anyhow?'

Roberts doubled his legs and pushed restlessly against
the top bunk. 'What's the matter with Stupid?' he
mused. 'Oh, mostly that — that he *is* stupid. Downright
low intelligence — that, coupled with a great deal of
vanity. Also he suffers from infantilism.'

'What's that?' Pulver asked immediately, and when
Roberts told him he wanted to know: 'Is that what
makes him buy a commander's cap and keep it up
there?'

'Maybe,' Roberts said disinterestedly.

'Do you think he'll ever make commander?'

Roberts kicked the top bunk sharply. 'Absolutely not!'

Ensign Pulver rubbed his nose again. 'Say,' he said with sudden excitement, 'now's the time to throw that commander hat over the side! While the Old Man's at the movies!'

Roberts shook his head.

'Hey, sure,' Pulver insisted. 'Now's a wonderful time! Come on! How about it!'

Roberts shook his head again. 'You do it,' he said flatly. 'I'm comfortable here. Besides,' he added, 'I've got a better idea.'

'What's that?' Pulver asked quickly.

Roberts turned and smiled benignly at him. 'Let's have one of your beers.'

Ensign Pulver shook his head disappointedly. 'Can't,' he said. 'I only got six bottles left and I'm saving them.'

'What do you think you're saving them for?'

A look of cunning came into Pulver's face. 'Special occasions,' he grinned.

'I see,' said Roberts. 'And when do you expect the next special occasion?'

Pulver thought this over. 'Mothers' Day,' he announced. 'Come around Mothers' Day and we'll have a special occasion.'

'Do you know,' Roberts said sternly, 'what the government does with hoarders?'

Pulver grinned hugely and nodded.

'Do you know,' Roberts pursued, 'that if you covet material goods you can never enter the Kingdom of Heaven?'

Pulver grinned even more.

'Besides,' Roberts pointed out warningfully, 'one of these days while you're hoarding beer this ship is going to take a bomb or a torpedo. Then nobody'll get any good out of your lousy beer!'

Ensign Pulver shook his head and grinned craftily. 'No, it ain't,' he said happily. 'The Japs won't bother this bucket. They know an ally when they see one.'

Roberts shook his head sadly and rolled over on his side. 'That's disgusting treasonous talk,' he said. 'Throw me that tinfoil over there.' He pointed at a large ball on the desk.

Pulver got up obediently. 'That's not tinfoil,' he said. 'That's leadfoil.' He handed the ball to Roberts.

'Whatever it is, it's heavy,' Roberts said. 'Now give me a thick rubber band.'

Pulver did that too, unquestioningly.

Roberts picked off a small lump of leadfoil and kneaded it. 'Now turn around,' he ordered.

Pulver did that, too, and Roberts made a V of the rubber band, inserted the ball of leadfoil, and shot Pulver in the left buttock. Ensign Pulver jumped well clear of the deck. 'Ouch!' he yelled. 'Jesus Christ!' He rubbed fiercely at his pants.

'That hurt?' Roberts asked kindly.

Ensign Pulver said that it did.

'Say,' said Roberts, twirling the rubber band, 'there's something for you to do. Why don't you take some of this leadfoil and go shoot the Old Man in the buttocks now while he's watching the movie?'

Pulver sat down in the chair again, and now he looked up quickly, interested but skeptical. His voice was carefully determined not to show enthusiasm. 'You come along,' he said, 'and I will.'

'No, no,' said Roberts solemnly, 'that's ridiculous. I won't be a party to anything like that. I think the Old Man is a lovable old gent. Beneath that rough exterior' — Roberts rapped on the bunk for emphasis — 'beats a heart of gold. Remember that.'

Ensign Pulver was not impressed. 'Come on,' he said earnestly, 'let's go do that. Come on,' he said, 'that's a good idea. Let's go do it!' He was getting a little excited.

Roberts turned over and laughed. 'No, no, no,' he said. 'Don't be silly. A man in my position.'

Pulver was pleading now. 'Come on, Doug,' he urged. 'Come on. Let's go do that. That'll be wonderful! Come on!'

Roberts shook his head adamantly and smiled. 'Out of the question,' he said flatly. He threw his leg over the side of the bunk and sat up. 'Okay,' he said, 'get the leadfoil and let's go.'

The snipers chose as their place of concealment the port wing of the boat deck. Ensign Pulver was giggling excitedly as they crowded in close against the bulkhead of the house. It was an ideal place: it was dark on the wing and there was no one about. The officers sat directly below on the quarterdeck, and the Captain, seated prominently in the center, was about twenty feet to the right. Roberts leaned over the rail and looked at the crowd. Everyone was intently watching the movie. It was evidently a thrilling moment, for a furious chase by horseback was in progress and the sound track was thunderous with horses' hooves and shouts and gunshots. The Captain was leaning avidly forward and his mouth was open with excitement. Leaning forward like that, Roberts noted, away from the back of the chair, the Captain presented a considerable expanse of buttock.

'All right,' Roberts said quietly to Pulver. 'You can have the first shot.'

Ensign Pulver, although not normally so, was brave enough with Roberts behind him. 'Okay,' he whispered tensely. 'Here I go!' He pulled back the rubber band and held it for a long moment, aiming. His hands were a little unsteady with excitement. Then he sucked in his breath and let fire. Immediately he ducked his head below the level of the rail and crouched there, waiting. When, after a moment, there were no sounds from below, he peered furtively over. The big pursuit was still going on, and none of the audience had so much as moved an eye.

'Let me try it,' Roberts said. He moved in close to the bulkhead. In naval gunfire, the term 'ballistic' is used to designate the completed computation — with corrections for wind, pitch and roll, gun-barrel thread, etc. — of the target range and bearing. Roberts figured his ballistic now. He made a small correction to the right for a very slight movement of air. He made a small correction upward on the theory that the leadfoil pellet would travel in a downward parabola. Then he took quick aim and fired. It was immediately apparent that he had figured the ballistic correctly.

The men at the movie thought the Captain had finally gone off his nut. (Indeed, until the explanation was thoroughly disseminated, this impression persisted for several days.) The Captain jumped up out of his chair just as though he'd been shot. At first he just cursed incoherently and then he started running around his chair and shouting, 'Stop the picture! Goddamit, stop the picture, I say!' Then all of a sudden he ran like a streak to the port side of the quarterdeck and peered aft. Then he ran over to the starboard side and did the same thing. And then, most inexplicably of all, he grabbed the handle of the general alarm at the starboard gangway and sounded General Quarters.

The crew never did understand it that night. They went bewilderedly but excitedly to their battle stations and as soon as they got there they heard the Captain's raging voice on the P.A. system.

'All right now, by God, we'll just stay right here at G.Q. until the smart son-of-a-bitch who did that comes up here and owns up! We'll stay right here, by God!'

The crew standing at their stations on the guns and in the engine room and on the bridge couldn't figure what had happened. Either somebody had done something to the Old Man, or he had completely lost his marbles: and in either case it was all right with the crew. They stood at their stations mystified, but gratified and excited, and considering the two probabilities they would willingly have stayed there all night. The movie had been lousy anyhow. The Captain got on the P.A. system twice more and said substantially what he had said before; and then, after forty-five minutes and still without explanation, the ship secured from General Quarters.

Ensign Pulver's battle station was in the engine room, and when he came up he found Roberts in the passageway outside the wardroom. Roberts was in a group with Langston and Billings, and Ensign Pulver heard him asking earnestly: 'What the hell happened anyway?'

Pulver waited until the group dispersed and then, grinning like an arch-conspirator, he grabbed Roberts's arm.

'Nice going!' he said impulsively. 'Man, oh man, that was nice going!'

Roberts disengaged himself coolly from Pulver's clutch. He eyed Pulver as though he were a total stranger. Then a swift glitter of something like cognizance came into his eyes. 'Say,' he said decisively, 'What do you say we have a beer now? This ought to be a special occasion.'

Ensign Pulver hesitated for just the barest instant, then he said warmly: 'Sure, come on! This *is* a special occasion!' He grinned at Roberts and his eyes were wide with helpless admiration.

Nothing in ensign keith's background and early training had adequately conditioned him for duty aboard the *Reluctant*. He was not a prude, but, coming from a middle-class family of a Boston suburb, he had deeply acquired a certain correctness of out-

look which resembled prudishness, and which, for
a time, warred vigorously with his new milieu. From
early Bostonian childhood he had been taught that
certain truths were self-evident: that the Demo-
cratic Party was incorrigibly evil; that a long engage-
ment was essential to a happy marriage; that solitary
drinking makes a drunkard; and that breeding and
character were what counted in life. When he had
finished two years at Bowdoin, the Navy came along,
made him an officer and issued him a few more Truths:
that an officer was, *ipso facto*, a gentleman; that a commission in the Navy was a sacred trust; that an officer
must not fraternize with enlisted men; and the one to
the effect that an officer enjoys special privileges by
virtue of his added responsibilities. Young Keith came
aboard equipped with a full set of these excellent, if
sometimes impractical Truths, and it took Dowdy and
the boys the better part of a month to get, as Dowdy
put it, 'Mr. Keith squared away.'

His arrival on board the *Reluctant*, or rather the
manner of it, was a genuine event. It was discussed in
the wardroom and the messhall and the engineroom for
months, and it is not likely to be forgotten within the
lifetime of any member of the ship's company. Keith
caught the ship while it lay at anchor in the bay of
Tedium Island. The day was typically hot and sticky,
and the lightest shirt was uncomfortable. The Captain
was ashore, and the gangway watch had relaxed accordingly. Ed Pauley, the officer-of-the-deck, was sitting
on a bitt reading an Ellery Queen story, and Farns-

worth, the messenger, was poring over a comics book when Farnsworth glanced over the side and saw this most remarkable thing. A boat from the beach was making the gangway and an officer, lugging heavy baggage, was climbing aboard. Neither the arrival of the boat nor of an officer with baggage was necessarily remarkable, but the officer himself was spectacularly so: he was wearing blues! 'Holy Jesus!' croaked Farnsworth, 'Mr. Pauley!'

Pauley got to his feet just in time to see a young ensign stand rigidly at the head of the gangway, salute the colors, step aboard, salute him and announce with great positiveness: 'Request permission to come aboard, sir. Ensign Keith reporting for duty.' The face of Ensign Keith, whose cheeks were perhaps naturally rosy, was now a fiery red and streaming with perspiration; at his armpits and at his back wide black stains were spreading, his trousers hung like wet washrags, and his white shirt was sweated to a solid gray. In a kind of trance Pauley, who was wearing faded khakis, dirty trousers, almost buttonless shirt open at the neck and torn down the sleeve, returned the salute and mumbled, 'Sure, sure . . . My name's Pauley.' It took Pauley a minute or two to collect himself, and then he led the new arrival in to see the executive officer.

Mr. LeSueur was an outspoken man. He was sitting at his desk when Pauley, trailed by Keith, appeared. For a moment he just stared, popeyed; then, before Pauley could say a word, before Keith could even state his business, he shouted: 'What in the hell are you doing in those things?' You could hear him far down the passageway.

Ensign Keith was visibly upset. At midshipmen's school they had taught that reporting aboard ship was a very formal business; they had never even intimated that he might be greeted like this. 'I'm Ensign Keith,' he said as well as he could. 'Reporting for duty, sir.'

Mr. LeSueur pounded the desk. 'That doesn't answer my question! What in the hell are you doing in blues?'

Ensign Keith, who was standing at rigid attention, turned even redder. 'When reporting for duty, blue baker is the uniform prescribed by Navy Regs, sir,' he said stiffly.

Mr. LeSueur passed a hand over his face. 'Blue baker,' he muttered. 'Navy Regs.' Finally he got up and shook hands with Keith. 'And for Christ's sake get out of those things in a hurry!' he told him. He turned to Pauley: 'Take him to your room, Ed. You'll live with Mr. Pauley.' Without another word he sat down and returned to his work.

Ensign Keith lingered uncertainly in the doorway. He licked his lips. 'Sir,' he said weakly, 'when shall I meet the Captain?'

Mr. LeSueur turned around with fearsome self-control. 'In the morning,' he said. 'I'll take you up there in the morning.'

'Thank you, sir,' said Keith. Still he lingered. At midshipmen's school they had taught that you must send your card up to the Captain. He wasn't quite sure with whom you sent it up; he thought it was probably the executive officer. He fumbled in his pockets. 'Will you give him my card, sir?'

Then Mr. LeSueur was shouting again. 'Card! Card! What the hell would he do with a card! The stupid bastard can't even read! Card!' Pauley grabbed Ensign Keith and led him hurriedly off, and when they got to the room they could still hear: 'Card! Card!' The interview hadn't gone at all the way it was supposed to.

If the way to enter cold water is to dive head-first, then perhaps Ensign Keith's ungentle immersion into his new life was for the best. Perhaps it had the virtue of numbing him against the shocks to follow. Certainly there were plenty of them. In the next few days he was buffeted with surprises like a non-stop punching bag. Almost everything he saw and heard, contradicted, refuted, ignored, or scorned one of the impregnable Truths he had learned so well. His new roommate, Ed Pauley, didn't get up at seven o'clock, when an officer should; he slept until noon. He didn't shave daily as an officer should; he was growing a shaggy red beard. The officers lounged all day in the sacrosanct wardroom. They kept their hats on in the wardroom, a scandalous violation of naval etiquette. Some of them even sat with their feet on the tables. None of them seemed to do any work. None used the title 'sir' in addressing each other, but other more vigorous and colloquial titles were freely used. Coarse, extra-marital exploits were discussed openly at the dinner-table. Some of the officers drank; Keith was sure he had

smelled liquor on Ed Pauley's breath, and fairly sure he
had smelled it on the Doctor. He had heard any
number of the officers addressing the enlisted men by
their first names, or by nicknames. With his own ears
he had heard various officers speak seditiously of the
ship and the Navy and, worst of all, of the Captain.
He had even heard one officer, this Ensign Pulver,
threaten in a convincing voice to commit a piece of
shocking mischief against the Captain. And they didn't
refer to him as the Captain at all; they called him
'Stupid.' Or worse than that.

Young Keith was shocked; he was shocked. He could
scarcely have been more shaken had his own mother
gone out and robbed the Kenmore Trust and Savings.
In all of his twenty and a half years nothing like this
had ever happened. Everything had always come off
in good order: the planets had stayed in their orbits;
once a week, before Sunday dinner, his mother had
served the family one Martini; a really well-mannered
girl didn't swear; and people — one's own kind, that is —
were always nice and considerate and well-bred. Life
revolved smoothly about certain fixed and astral values
and intangibles; things like character and family and
the Episcopal Church, things whose sanctity it would
be insane even to question. And when he joined
the Navy, Keith had added another: the Navy.
Now, suddenly, these untouchables were not only
handled, they were mauled; they were assaulted
continually. When a thing like that happens, when

the roots of a man's faith are torn out and examined, he can do one of two things: he can bind them to himself all the more fiercely, or he can let them go. For a few days Ensign Keith was very quiet, and it wasn't clear which course he would take. Then, consciously or not, he seemed to make a decision.

The first time Keith stood a watch, it became clear which way he would go. It was Dowdy, the boatswain's mate, who brought this to light. Dowdy was over on the beach one day, ostensibly on ship's business. Actually he had another purpose. He had heard of a Seabee who would part with beer for a price. This Seabee wanted, and got, two dollars a bottle, and Dowdy bought six bottles which he concealed delicately in the only cardboard box available, one which bore the startling label 'Kotex.' Dowdy wondered for a while where the hell that box came from and then, on the way back to the ship, he quit thinking about the box and began thinking of the beer. It had been four months since he had had beer, and he thought with almost unbearable affection of his cargo. When he got back aboard, he knew exactly what he would do: he would get a bucket, fill it with ice from the galley, lock himself in the boatswain's locker and wait for the beer to cool, and then drink it all, every lovely bottle. Maybe he would give one bottle to his friend Olson, the first-class gunner's mate. He considered this as he trudged up the gangway.

As he stepped aboard, he threw the usual perfunctory salute to the colors and started aft. He noticed, more or less in passing, the officer-of-the-deck — it was that new kid, what was his name? — but he didn't bother saluting. Dowdy was pretty much of a personage on the ship, and all the officers either respected him or left him alone. He had gotten perhaps ten feet when he heard someone call: 'Where do you think you're going?' and he turned around and saw this boot ensign standing there, giving him the dirtiest kind of look. Dowdy was all set to put the kid in his place, but before he could say a word, Ensign Keith shot a question that absolutely floored him: 'How long have you been in the Navy?'

Well, Dowdy had eleven years in, and to hear this question from the mouth of a brand-new ensign was too much. Dowdy was too flabbergasted to speak. He just stood there and his mouth worked like a fish and no sound came out.

'When you come aboard you salute the officer-of-the-deck,' Ensign Keith explained acidly. 'Now go back and come aboard properly!'

It was a moment before Dowdy could even move. Then in a kind of idiotic sleepwalk he went back and came aboard properly: he saluted Ensign Keith.

'That's better,' said Ensign Keith bitingly. 'Watch it after this.' He looked Dowdy up and down coldly. He noticed the box under Dowdy's arm. 'What's that?' he asked suspiciously.

Dowdy stared stupidly at the box, as though seeing it for the first time. He got his voice back now, but his thinking remained stalled. 'That's Kotex,' he said.

'They use it down in sick-bay.' It wasn't a very likely story.

'Let me see,' said Ensign Keith. And Dowdy's will was so paralyzed that he handed him the priceless box, a thing he never would have done in his right mind.

Ensign Keith tore open the box. Then his eyes went wide and his voice got shrill. 'Beer!' he shouted. 'Beer! Bringing liquor on board a Navy ship! Don't you know that's a general court-martial offense? How long have you been in the Navy anyhow?' And before Dowdy's helpless, pleading, agonized eyes he flung the box over the side. The gift of movement returned to Dowdy then, and he rushed to the rail just in time to witness a scene of incredible waste: six bottles of irreplaceable beer sinking in eight fathoms of water. The sight brought tears to his eyes. For a brief, burning moment of insanity, he thought of strangling Ensign Keith; but his will for even that pleasurable task was gone before he could act. A broken man, Dowdy stumbled off to the compartment. It would take him hours and maybe days to figure out what had hit him. A boot ensign! Dowdy felt like crying.

Young Keith's reputation was made right there. From the obscure 'new ensign' he was transformed overnight into the best-known officer on the ship. News of the gangway incident spread like a kerosene fire: let alone, it would certainly have attained a fabulous, legendary character; it was the most startling thing to happen in months. But Ensign Keith didn't let it stand alone; he added to it. He added to it the very next morning when he put the messenger on report for sneaking below to smoke without his permission. He added to it that same afternoon when he put two men on report for appearing on deck without their shirts — a foolish requirement of the Captain's which no one had ever attempted to enforce. Every day and every way he added to it. At sea, standing junior O.O.D. watches, he insisted that the gun crews stay on their feet; and two more men went on report for sitting on a ready box. Dolan, the second-class quartermaster, talked back to him and made the report list. Steuben, the yeoman, made it by appearing two minutes late to relieve the watch. The report list was no longer an exclusive thing. Twelve cases appeared before Captain's mast one Saturday, and for ten of them Ensign James L. Keith was the complaining witness. He was hell on wheels. He seemed to be trying, singlehanded, to atone for the laxity of the rest of the ship. In port, on his watch, he required every man who approached the quarterdeck to salute him and state his business. He banished all reading matter from the gangway desk. He demanded that his messengers stand their watches in immaculate dungarees. He seemed to be trying, singlehanded, to restore the ship to the Navy, from whence it had strayed.

One morning in port on the four-to-eight watch he decided that the crew wasn't turning out for reveille. He was very right. Chief Johnson made reveille at six-thirty and at a quarter of seven Ensign Keith went down in the compartment and found it loaded with sleeping

bodies. He summoned his most resolute voice and addressed the bodies: 'All right! Get up here! Get out
of those sacks. Every man who's not out of here in five
minutes goes on report!' Not a sound. Not a movement. Here and there an eyelid cracked ever so slightly
to peer at the intruder; that was all. Suddenly from the
far, after corner of the compartment a clear, unstutter-
ing voice sounded: 'Get out of here, you son-of-a-bitch.
I'm warning you!' Dowdy lived in that corner, but the
voice could have been anyone's. Ensign Keith jumped.
'Who said that?' he demanded weakly. Silence. Heavy
breathing. Not a movement. Ensign Keith repeated
his previous threat: 'I'll be back here in five minutes.
Everyone who's not out goes on report.' It didn't sound
at all convincing. He didn't come back either.

A wise man would have profited from that experience, and perhaps it left a mark on young Ensign
Keith; but nothing that was immediately apparent. He
went on much as before, only he didn't try to make a
personal reveille again. The report list stayed as long
as ever. He gave the crew a thoroughly bad time. If
he were embarked upon a deliberate program of self-
destruction, he could not have chosen a more likely
means to achieve his end. He became the object and
the focus and the intention of a quite terrifying pitch
of hatred. He had strayed onto an area which few of
the officers ever violated, a buffer area of good feeling
between officers and men constructed painstakingly of
mutual tolerance, compromise, and tacit understanding.
The officers left the men alone and the men did the

same: that way both were free to concentrate upon the Captain. Ensign Keith not only trespassed on that area, he stomped all over it. In a very short time the feeling against him competed favorably with that against the Captain, and it wasn't long until the Captain was completely outstripped and relegated to the rôle of second-rate enemy. Considering Ensign Keith, one man, Ludlow, a first division coxswain, was even moved to speak these treasonous words: 'You know the Old Man ain't so bad.' He was hushed up before any real damage could be done, but the fact remained that young Keith put the Captain in a very favorable light. The compartment at night buzzed with talk of the new ensign, and in the dark corners little sinister groups would gather and plot and threaten and scheme. A quite wise man, Dowdy, listened to this talk and gauged it, and when he became convinced of its serious intent, he went to his friend, Lieutenant Roberts: 'Mr. Roberts,' he said, 'if he doesn't knock it off, that new ensign is going to wake up some day with a marlinspike through his skull. Can you pound some sense in his head? The boys down there are really getting to feel mean.' Roberts promised to talk with Ensign Keith.

The talk wasn't very successful. Roberts found Keith alone in his room and in a very nice, tactful way tried to explain a few things. He was very decent about it. He pointed out that, for such a ship, Keith was being unnecessarily regulation. He pointed out that Keith was making a great many enemies, and that, in a small, interdependent community like this it wasn't a good idea to have too many enemies. Then he asked Keith very politely if he didn't think he could ease up just a little.

Ensign Keith listened with the respect due his senior officer, then he answered formally: 'I appreciate your interest, sir, but I feel that I'm just doing my duty. The regulations which I'm trying to enforce were made by the fathers of our Navy and they've lasted a long time. I feel that there must be a reason for them and, as a naval officer, it's a matter of conscience with me to see that they're obeyed. After all,' he finished loftily, 'a man's first duty is to his conscience.'

You really couldn't argue with such moral superiority, but Roberts did his best. 'Yes,' he said, 'I don't doubt that they're excellent regulations on a combatant ship. But on a ship like this they're just not very practical. On this ship you have to depend on co-operation to a great extent. There's a good bunch on here, and I think you'll find that, if you just give them a break, treat them decently, don't push them around, they'll do anything you ask. Why don't you give it a try?'

Ensign Keith regarded him coldly. 'I'm sorry, sir,' he said, 'but I don't believe in fraternization. I believe,' he said with finality, 'that familiarity breeds contempt.'

That was the failure of mediation, and Ensign Keith continued on his implacable way. It seemed then that there was no solution short of the marlinspike. His case looked hopeless, and it looked black. The mutterings grew louder and bolder in the dark corners of the compartment. His life expectancy dropped lower and lower, and just when it seemed nil, a solution came to pass of such aptness, happiness, and general satisfaction that Ensign Keith was completely forgiven his transgressions and restored in full standing to the community of good-will, from which he never strayed again. It happened one night at sea.

Under way, young Keith stood junior O.O.D. watches under Ed Pauley. The J.O.O.D. was the battery officer and he was also, nominally, the security officer. He was presumed, at least once a watch, to make the rounds of the ship and determine that everything was safe, peaceful, and reasonably quiet. The other J.O.O.D.'s frequently left the bridge on security patrol, but the only place they ever visited was the wardroom, where they investigated the quality of the coffee. Ensign Keith examined every corner of the ship. On this night he was standing the eight-to-twelve watch with Pauley. It was perhaps ten o'clock when he left the bridge to make the rounds. He went through the compartment, through the galley and the messhall, around past the refrigeration spaces and the storerooms and the offices, down into the 'tween-decks spaces along the starboard side and back again on the port side, past more storerooms and the barber shop and the armory. At the armory he stopped. A crack of light was showing under the door, and inside he could hear voices and a rattling sound. There was a funny smell, too. Ensign Keith pushed the door open.

A startled group looked up at him from the deck. Dowdy was there, and Olson, and Dolan, and Vanessi, the storekeeper, and Stefanowski, the machinist's mate, and over in the corner by the rifle racks, holding a glass in one hand and with the other trying to force a record onto the turntable of the portable phonograph was Schaffer, another gunner's mate. The air in the armory was thick with smoke and this other smell. On the deck beside Olson was a large pewter crock from the galley, and the men had glasses beside them. The group on the deck was huddled kneeling before the after bulkhead, and Dowdy had just thrown a pair of dice against the bulkhead. Each man had a pile of bills beside him, and in the middle of the cleared space there were other piles.

Ensign Keith shut the door behind him. He looked quickly and accusingly around the room. 'You men are gambling,' he announced.

No one spoke. No one affirmed or denied the charge. No one moved. Six pairs of sullen, menacing eyes watched Ensign Keith.

'Don't you know,' he demanded, 'that gambling is a general court-martial offense?'

A look of craftiness came to Dowdy's face. 'Oh, we ain't gambling, sir,' he said kindly, as though Keith had made a perfectly natural mistake. 'We're just shooting a little crap for fun. It's not for money.'

'Then what's the money doing out there?' Keith asked triumphantly.

Dowdy smiled and dismissed it with his hand. 'Oh, that's just to keep score with. We figure out that way who has the most points and then at the end of the game we give it all back.' He smiled disarmingly at the officer. 'It's the best way I've found yet to keep score.' He added righteously, 'No, sir, we can't none of us afford to gamble. We've found that gambling never pays.'

Ensign Keith stood there, doubt and anger and uncertainty chasing each other across his face. He lifted his cap and replaced it on his head. He pinched his nose. He looked suspiciously around the room and saw the glasses and the pewter crock, and he smelled the funny smell.

'What's that?' he demanded. 'In that jar there? What are you drinking?'

Dowdy looked over at the crock. 'That?' he said soothingly. 'Oh, that's some fruit juice. That's some pineapple juice we got from the galley. That's all that is.'

Ensign Keith wasn't satisfied. 'Let me see,' he said to Olson.

Olson shot a quick, questioning glance at Dowdy.

Dowdy smiled benevolently. 'Sure,' he said. 'Give Mr. Keith a drink of fruit juice. Here's a glass.'

At any given time there were apt to be brewing on the ship fifteen different batches of jungle juice, but it was agreed that Olson made the most distinctive brand. His jungle juice had *character*, everyone said. For one thing, through influential connections among the mess cooks, he had access to more ingredients than his competitors. Olson would take an empty ten-gallon water breaker, fill it half-up with raisin mash, add what-

ever fruit juices — orange, pineapple, grapefruit, it
didn't matter — the mess cooks had been able to pro-
vide, add sugar, stir well, and stow the breaker in an
unlikely corner of number two hold. After a week to
ten days of turmoil, the mixture was ready for tapping.
It was as unpredictable as a live volcano. In taste, it
was as deceptively tranquil as sloe gin, and one or two
glasses would creep up on the uninitiated like a well-
wielded hand-billy. The night Biddle, the butcher, ran
amuck and tried to 'kill all the Guinnies' with a meat-
cleaver, he had been prodded by several glasses of
Olson's jungle juice.

It was ten o'clock when Ensign Keith left the bridge.
At eleven, Ed Pauley had occasion to call the flying
bridge, and Keith's absence was reported to him.
Pauley was irritated, but more than irritated he was
surprised that Keith was doping off: it wasn't at all
consistent. He sent the messenger around to find Keith,
and when, after a thorough fifteen-minute search the
messenger reported negatively, he became slightly
worried. He considered the vigorous feeling against
Keith. He remembered the threats he had heard. He
wondered if it wasn't just possible that something had
happened. He thought about this, and the more he
thought, the more plausible it seemed. He sent the messenger out again, and the messenger returned with the
same report. Eleven-forty-five and Ensign Mulholland
arrived to relieve Keith. Now Pauley was really
alarmed. He could visualize Keith swimming far back
there in the desolate wake, the sharks following at a

respectful distance. For a frantic moment he thought of calling the Captain — after all, the thing had happened on his watch — and then he controlled himself. He had best be sure first; he would search the ship himself; he would look in every goddamn *conceivable* place.

When Lieutenant Carney relieved him, he took Bergstrom, his quartermaster, and set out. Bergstrom carried a flashlight. Pauley fully expected to find Keith down in the bilges with a marlinspike in his back — if he found him at all. First they exhausted the likely places; all the officers' staterooms, radio room, offices, engineroom, heads. Then they started on the infinite number of unlikely places which, the way Pauley figured it, were really the probable ones. They went through the crew's compartment and looked in every bunk. They opened storerooms and even opened the refrigerator spaces. They looked in the Chief's quarters. They looked in the boatswain's locker. They even looked in the spud locker. Glumly, Pauley led the way through the 'tween-decks spaces on his way to the holds. This was a hell of a thing. If he didn't find him in the holds, he'd have to call the Old Man. There'd be hell to pay for this. As he passed the armory, Pauley heard music and voices. He stopped, for the loudest of the voices was clearly Keith's.

Pauley had prepared himself for almost anything, but not for what he found in the armory. Dowdy and Keith and Olson were standing against the workbench. Dowdy and Olson had their arms flung about Keith, simultaneously supporting him and leaning on him.

Loudly and with much stress on certain words the three were singing a thoroughly obscene tune called 'Violate me in the Violet time in the Vil-est way that you know.' Within the compass of his two supporters, Keith was flopping his arms about to no discernible rhythm. His eyes were glassy and a huge white grin was pasted on his face. The phonograph beside them was unobtrusively playing a Strauss waltz. Over by the bulkhead Vanessi and Stefanowski teetered on their haunches and peered nearsightedly at the dice on the deck. They argued noisily about what the dice read. In the corner, lying on his back, cradled on two life jackets, Schaffer slept soundly. His mouth was open and a marshmallow was propped in it. There were at least two broken glasses on the deck and the air was fragrant with the smell of jungle juice. Everyone, less Schaffer, greeted Pauley hilariously.

When he had recovered a little, Pauley pointed at Keith: 'Who's that?' he asked.

Dowdy peered into Keith's face to find out. He shook him by the shoulder and Keith's head bobbed back and forth. 'That?' said Dowdy. 'That's old Jim Keith. You know old Jim Keith.'

Keith nodded his head solemnly and grinned some more. 'This is old Jim Keith,' he echoed. 'You know old Jim Keith.'

Dowdy winked widely at Pauley. He continued to shake Keith's shoulder. 'Yessir,' he announced, 'old Jim's a good son-of-a-bitch.'

Keith nodded heavy approval. 'Yessir,' he mumbled.

'Old Jim's a good son-of-a-bitch.' Then without a sound, a surprised look on his face, as though the idea had just occurred to him, he slipped easily to the deck, sound asleep.

It turned out he was right about being a good son-of-a-bitch. His old rectitude collapsed like a pricked balloon. He never gave the boys trouble again. He took to sleeping until noon and sitting around the wardroom with his feet in bedroom slippers propped on a table. Until the Captain put a stop to it, he wore for a while a tan polo shirt that was screamingly non-regulation. He and his messenger would spend the gangway watches playing checkers on a miniature board, and at sea Keith would sit on a ready box and listen to the stories that fanned from his gun crews. He turned out to be a nice, good-natured kid. As Dowdy said, it just took a little while to get him squared away.

T HE DOCTOR WAS VARIOUSLY DESCRIBED as a crazy little bastard, a son-of-a-bitch, a good son-of-a-bitch, a hell of a good medico, a quack from the word go, and a nice guy. The area of agreement in all these estimates is that the Doc was contradictory and unpredictable. The Doc was that. The story went that, on the outside, he had held a lucrative Hollywood practice, but he didn't look the part. Doc was rather a plump little man, balding, in his middle thirties; and if it is true that humans always resemble some animal type, then perhaps he most suggested an outsized, juicy, cherubic mouse — with certain qualifications. The qualifications being really contradictions and most unmouselike, the comparison doesn't mean much. The contradictions were the face and the man — the satanic little mustache, the wide, unblinking eyes that were simultaneously cruel and compassionate, the shockingly soft voice that never quite concealed the steel beneath. Among the crew he seemed to inspire two antagonistic feelings in equal degree: fear, and a rather boundless admiration. Anyone who had ever drawn the wrath of his sharp little tongue had good cause to hold the Doc in respect, but on the other hand there were many whose relations with him had been of the friendliest sort imaginable. The pharmacist's mates, who had cause to feel both ways, swore by him, and would have, even if he did not, as he did, crack a frequent bottle of grain alcohol with them.

There wasn't really much call for a doctor on the ship and the Doc had little to do. Most of the time he sat in his room, working advanced calculus problems, reading Nietzsche or Schopenhauer, or talking with anyone who chanced in the doorway. Once a day, at eight-thirty in the morning, he held sick call. The attendance at sick call would vary from time to time, but the

complaints — the legitimate ones, that is — seldom did.
For all practical purposes, such as codification, there
were only three: constipation, fungus infection, and
what the Navy calls cat fever. Once in a while there
would be boils needing lancing, a case of appendicitis
and maybe even an appendectomy, or simple lacera-
tions such as might be produced by a fist, but by and
large all complaints fell into the conventional and approved diagnoses. The attendance was not so uniform,
and seemed to be subject to various irrelevant influ-
ences. On a holiday routine (with sleeping-in au-
thorized) never would more than a handful turn out.
But the very next day — if the day called for a vigorous
program of chipping and scraping decks — might see a
queue extending all the way to the galley lined up in
the passageway outside of sick-bay. Any other medical
man than the Doc would have been amazed that such
a number of cases, and such acute ones, of hangnail,
hernia, stomach ulcers, mastoiditis, piles, and strep
throat could develop overnight. It had been a long
time since anything had amazed the Doc, but every
once in a while he had to own himself impressed at the
imaginativeness of the sick-call complaints. He was
certainly impressed when, on a day the first division
was scheduled to paint over the side, Farnsworth, a
first division man, announced that he thought he was
coming down with Huntington's chorea, a disease of
such rarity as to constitute a medical phenomenon.
When Biddle, the butcher, took his meat-cleaver and
made realistic attempts to 'kill all the Guinnies' on the

ship, the Doc transferred him to an island hospital with
a diagnosis of war neurosis and excellent prospects for
a medical survey. At sick-call next morning five new
cases made their appearance, and it took the Doc a
week to stamp out the epidemic of war neuroses which
suddenly flourished on the ship.

There was one time, one sick-call, when the Doc was
indisputably amazed. It happened, too, on a morning
when he was physiologically not quite equal to amaze-
ment. For a week the ship had been anchored in the
bay of this rank, weedy, desolate little island, and still
there were no prospects of early departure. Quite a
palpable depression was beginning to settle on the
crew, who agreed to a man that this was the most
miserable island of them all, and whose testimony on
the subject of miserable islands was irrefutably competent. There was a small Army base ashore, a smaller
Naval base, a dirty little native village unmolestedly off
by itself, and excessive quantities of mud and dust and
jungle and smell: that was all. It was truly the end of
the world. Like everyone else, the Doc had fallen prey
to the smothering depression that emanated from the
place, and the night before he had taken practical
remedial measures: he had depleted the medicine
locker by one quart of one-hundred-fifty proof, government specification grain alcohol, which he shared
with Lieutenant Roberts and Ed Pauley. Grain alcohol
and orange juice make a pleasing but not very gentle
drink, and this morning Doc had an active headache
and a tendency to impatience. Attended by Lupich,

the first-class pharmacist's mate, he disposed of the morning's turnout of hypochondriacs with immoral speed, issuing the blanket prescription of aspirin tablets for all complaints, including athlete's foot. 'You need an aspirin,' was his uniform diagnosis, and twice he added, 'See, I'll have one with you.'

Finally there was one man left: Lindstrom, a hulking, grinning seaman who lived up to every inch of the Dumb-Swede tradition. Lindstrom was a farmer boy from South Dakota, had a thatch of yellow hair that could easily have been straw, a hammered-down nose, wing-like ears, maddening good nature, and had once been summarized by Dowdy: 'When they were passing out brains, that son-of-a-bitch stepped out for a beer.' He had arrived early at sick-call and the Doc had noticed him moving back to the end of the line, repeatedly giving up his place to late-comers. Now he stood grinning awkwardly and flapping his cap up and down to no apparent purpose.

The Doc swiveled around in his chair and looked at him. 'What's your trouble?' he said coldly.

Lindstrom grinned some more, flapped his cap with one hand and scratched his head with the other, and finally said plaintively: 'I got the clap, Doc.'

The Doc was in no mood for phantasy. 'Don't be silly,' he snapped. 'Now what's the matter with you?'

Lindstrom kept grinning, shook his head doggedly and insisted: 'I got the clap, Doc.'

The Doc began to get angry. 'I said don't be silly! Where in the hell could you get the clap around here, boy?' He wasn't expecting any answer at all to that, and certainly not the one Lindstrom gave.

'Over on the beach, Doc. I was over on a working party the other day and this native guy, he took me up to his shack. This woman was there and I give her my knife and a pack of Chesterfields.' He was absorbedly shifting from one foot to the other, as though he had just discovered the gift of movement. 'She was pretty ugly,' he added pertinently.

The Doc's eyes were very wide. 'Come here,' he said quietly. He made his examination without a word. Then he turned around and stroked his mustache and regarded Lupich. 'Well, I'm a son-of-a-gun,' he said finally, and then, 'Well, lance me for a tiger.' He leaned back in the chair, joined his hands behind his head, and delivered a brief speech. 'Here,' he said, 'is a man who, on the most god-forsaken womanless island in the whole goddamn god-forsaken ocean, gets himself a dose of clap. That, I insist, is one for the medical journals. That is comparable to getting sunstroke in Alaska, or leprosy in Valhalla. I will write this up for the medical journals, furnish documented proof, and I will become famous.' He eyed Lindstrom. 'But not half so famous as you, young man.'

Lindstrom considered this speech dubiously. 'Yessir,' he said.

The Doc kept looking him over while he twisted the waxy villainous tips of his mustache. 'Well,' he said genially, 'you've got the clap. What do you come to me for?'

Lindstrom didn't find the question at all unreasonable. 'Well,' he explained obligingly, 'I thought maybe you could fix it up.'

'Fix it up?' The Doc's voice was incredulous. 'Do you mean cure it?' The cold, regarding eyes went wide in consternation.

The Swede was visibly unsettled. 'Yessir,' he said haltingly, the grin fading from his face. 'Can't you do that, Doc?'

'Why, of course I can do it. The simplest thing in the world! But you surely don't want me to. You're not serious, are you?'

The cap was flapping now in furious agitation, and on Lindstrom's face a sudden cloud of bewilderment had settled. 'Yessir,' he said apologetically. 'I'd kind of like to get rid of it if you could do it, Doc. I'd sure appreciate it.'

'Listen to me, son.' The Doc leaned forward earnestly and his voice purred with reasonableness. 'You don't want to get that cured and I'll tell you why.' He tapped the desk. 'How many men would you say there are out here in the Pacific?' he asked softly.

Lindstrom knotted his forehead, considering. 'There's a pile of them,' he said finally.

'Thousands?' the Doctor prodded. 'Would you say there were thousands?'

'Yeah, I guess so.'

'A million, perhaps? Would you say there were a million?'

'Yeah, I guess a million.'

'All right,' said the Doc. 'All right. Now there aren't many women out here, are there?'

The grin came back to Lindstrom's face. 'There ain't any, except for this gal over here!'

'All right,' the Doc said. 'All right. There aren't many chances to get the clap, then, are there?'

Lindstrom didn't guess there were.

'The clap must be pretty rare, then, among all these men, would you say?'

Lindstrom guessed it was.

'How many cases would you say there were?'

Lindstrom's brows were pulled down in a deep frown of concentration. He shuffled the floor. 'Not many,' he decided.

'Well, I'll tell you.' The Doc spoke with the coy self-gratulation of a man about to bestow a gift. 'I'll tell you. Yours is the only one. You have the only case. Out of the million men in this ocean, *you* have been chosen. You stand out.' He beamed almost pridefully at Lindstrom. 'Now what do you think of that?'

The Swede pawed the floor uncomfortably. 'Yessir,' he said.

'Do you see what I mean?' the Doc purred on. 'You are distinctive. You have something a million guys would give their left leg to have. You're the only one who has it. Now you surely don't want to lose it, do you?'

Lindstrom was trying to paw a hole through the deck and apparently so absorbed in the work that he couldn't answer.

'Let me put it this way,' the Doctor went on. 'If you had been awarded the Congressional Medal, you alone out of a million men, would you give it away?'

Lindstrom thought this over, and then he asked: 'What's the Congressional Medal?'

'That's the highest military decoration in the land. Would you give that away?'

The answers were clearly taped out for Lindstrom, but on this one he stepped outside the tapes. 'I'd give it to my old lady,' he said suddenly. He looked to the Doc for approval of this sentiment.

A faint little smile came to Doc's lips. 'The medal you mean, of course,' he said gently. 'Well, that would be nice. That would be a nice thought.' He sat quiet for a moment, as though he had lost the train of his argument. Then he resumed: 'But to get on with what I was saying, boy. You alone of one million men in this ocean have been blessed with the clap. Now when you go back to the States — where are you from, by the way . . . ?'

'Sir? Rapid City, South Dakota.'

'All right, when you go back to South Dakota, people are going to point you out and say: "The only man in the whole Pacific Ocean to get the clap, and he comes from our town! Why, I knew him when he was just a little boy!" You'll be just as good as a hero. You'll get your picture in the paper. You'll talk on the radio. They'll make a terrific fuss over you. Are you going to throw all that away?'

Lindstrom didn't seem to follow the argument. He said, 'Sir?'

'Do you want me to cure you?' the Doc paraphrased. 'Do you want to throw away your achievement, your medal, your distinction? Do you want to be clap-less like all the million other men out here?' He painted a metaphor: 'Do you want to be just another member of a mob scene or do you want to stand out? Which is it?'

Somehow — Lindstrom wasn't sure just how — the Doctor had conveyed in his talk the delicate threat that if his advice was disregarded it would be rank ingratitude; it would hurt the Doc. Lindstrom felt this and scratched his mop of hair and sought the softest words possible. 'Well, sir,' he said finally, 'I sure appreciate what you say and there's a lot in what you say, but all the same if you think it's okay I'd like to get cured.'

The Doctor looked sorrowfully over to Lupich. 'He wants to get cured.' He shrugged. 'All right,' he said. 'But be sure you know what you're saying. Don't do anything now that you're going to regret later. Maybe it would be a good idea if you slept on this thing and came back tomorrow with your decision. What do you think?'

Lindstrom saw that the suggestion was a good one and he considered it. He scratched some more. Then he said: 'No, sir, thanks all the same, but I don't figure I'll change my mind. I kind of think I'd like to get straightened out now.'

The Doc shrugged again in final defeat. 'All right,' he said sadly. 'You're the doctor.' He turned to Lupich. 'Sulfathiazole.'

When he left sick-bay that morning, Lindstrom was a quite disturbed and unhappy young man. For one thing, he knew that he had hurt the Doc. For another, he wasn't entirely certain that he had taken the right course. The Doc had sown doubt in his mind, and Lindstrom didn't quite have the equipment to put it out. He went and sat on a bitt on the fo'c'sle for a long time, reviewing the Doc's arguments and his own convictions, weighing them against each other. The more he thought about it, the more certain Lindstrom became that he had done the right thing. Just to be absolutely sure he decided to get Dowdy's opinion on it. Dowdy was his boss, the divisional leading petty officer, and Lindstrom, and better minds than Lindstrom's, considered him infallible.

He found Dowdy down in the boatswain's locker, splicing a section of wire cable. He told Dowdy the whole story, including the Doctor's arguments, and Dowdy didn't even look up from his work. As he talked on, it became more and more obvious to Lindstrom that he had done the right thing. He finished on a note of scornful superiority. 'And you know what? The Doc wanted me to keep the clap, he wanted me to keep it like a medal, he said. Hell, he's crazy, ain't he? Did you ever hear anything so crazy?' And Lindstrom laughed and slapped his knee and looked to Dowdy for confirmation.

He came to the wrong man. Without interrupting the delicate work, Dowdy said evenly: 'No, he's not crazy. He's absolutely right. You're the one that's crazy. You've got holes in your head if you get rid of the only dose of clap in the whole damn Pacific.'

Lindstrom was really unhappy then. It took him two full days of steady, torturous ratiocination to reconvince himself that he had made the right decision. And even then, whenever he saw Dowdy, he would feel stirring the pangs of doubt.

IT SEEMED TO LIEUTENANT ROBERTS that he had just fallen asleep when the flashlight shone in his face, awakening him for the watch. He had been dreaming and in his dream his dead mother was there; it was summer at his home and he was going out to play tennis. His mother was sitting on the porch drinking a Coca-Cola, and as he went out she said: 'On your way back pick up some pastry for supper.' And he got into the car and started off, and at the corner he smashed right into another car; and when the driver of the other car came toward him, he saw that it was Captain Morton. The flashlight shone questioningly in his face and he was fully awake by the time the messenger called: 'Mr. Roberts! Mr. Roberts! It's eleven-thirty, sir. You have the watch.'

Roberts put a hand to his eyes and rubbed them. 'Okay,' he said. 'Thank you.' The messenger went out, stumbling in the darkened stateroom against the chair. Carefully, he pulled the door to behind him; he knew that Mr. Roberts would get up; you only had to call Mr. Roberts once. Roberts lay on his back not moving a muscle, numbly, tiredness an actual ache in his legs, considering the fact that sleep was over and now for four hours — another four of the hours that wheeled past ceaselessly like ducks in a shooting gallery — he must get up and stand in the darkness. Here we go again, he thought; and as he lay there he felt the old incipient despair that for two hours he had eluded returning again. To stop it he stopped his mind; he had learned well how to do that. He lay there and all he was doing was breathing and listening. In the hot, pitch-dark little room there were four distinct sounds. There was the noisy breathing of Langston in the bunk above him — a long wheezing inspiration, then a pause, then a wet, angry snort. There was the hissing drone of the blower in the overhead and the whirring of the fan that wearily pushed the heavy air over to the bunks. Over on the desk the cheap alarm-clock ticked stridently. Roberts raised his head and looked at the luminous dial: eleven-thirty-five. He lay still a moment longer; then he stretched and sat up. In the darkness he reached to the deck and put on his stockings and shoes and still without turning on the light he found the rest of his clothes and put them on. As he went out he closed the door quietly, although he could have slammed it fifteen times without awakening Langston.

He went down to the wardroom, where one overhead light burned dimly. It was deserted; a few old and much-tumbled magazines were strewn about the tables. There was no one in the pantry either; not even the steward's mate with the watch. Incuriously, Roberts looked through the refrigerator for something to eat and, finding nothing, poured himself a cup of coffee from the Silex and sat down at a table. He picked up a six-months-old copy of *Time* and looked at the book section to see if he had read it. He had; he threw it aside. He drank the black coffee in deep swallows and felt better; it smothered some of the weariness, his legs felt better, he could stand the watch now. He stretched again, shook his head like a swimmer with water in his ear, put on his cap, and walked slowly up the two ladders to the charthouse. There he initialed the Captain's night-order book — always the same: 'Call me at any time if in doubt' — and looked at the chart. The closest land was four hundred miles. He went out into the wheelhouse.

Usually, before he took the officer-of-the-deck watch, Roberts would stand at night in the rear of the wheelhouse and let his eyes adjust to the darkness. Tonight, though, as soon as he stepped into the wheelhouse, he could see. A bright moonlight was streaming through the portholes and almost right away he could make out every object in the room and every person. He asked the helmsman: 'Where's Mr. Carney?' and the helmsman told him: 'Out on the port wing.' Roberts went out on the wing and found Carney leaning on the pelorus.

Like all watch-standers about to be relieved, Carney was jovial. 'Welcome,' he said. 'And good morning.'

Roberts smiled wryly. 'Good morning,' he said. He waited for Carney to give him the dope.

'Well,' Carney began, 'we're steaming along in this here ocean at ten knots, seventy-two r.p.m., and the base course is two-five-eight and that's what we're steering. No zigzag, no nothing; everything's peaceful.'

'I trust Stupid's gone to bed?' said Roberts.

'Stupid's gone to bed.'

'Okay,' said Roberts, 'anything else?'

'Nope, nothing else. No course changes.'

'Okay,' Roberts said. 'I've got it.'

'Okay.' Carney made a gestured salute. He stood around a moment, trying not to appear too anxious to go below. 'Hell of a bright night,' he said.

'It really is.'

Carney shifted his cap and yawned. 'Okay,' he said

vaguely. He slouched off into the charthouse to write his log and turn in.

Roberts had the watch. For maybe the thousandth time in two and a half years he had the watch. He stood alone on the wing and considered this fact. For a moment he thought of figuring just how many watches he had stood; then he gave it up. He pinched his eyes in an old nervous mannerism and got ready. This would be a long watch, the mid-watch always was; and besides, there was nothing doing, which made it worse. He might as well get the watch organized, get that over with. He looked into the gyro repeater and checked the course with the helmsman. He checked the gyro with the standard and steering compasses. He asked the talker if everyone had been relieved on the guns: they had been. He had the talker ask Radar if there was anything around: there wasn't. That squared away the watch. Now there was nothing to do, nothing at all to do but stay on the course, and a moron could do that.

He walked back to the wing, leaned against the windshield, and looked out at the sea and the night; and for the first time he noticed what an incredible night it was. The moon — what an enormous moon! It had risen yellow and round and fat, and now that it was higher it had shrunk a little, but still it was round and full, and no longer yellow, but molten, incandescent silver. The light it spread was daylight with the harshness filtered out, unbelievably pure and even and dimensionless. On the bridge you could have read a newspaper: it was that bright. The moon now was on the port quarter and all the way to the horizon it parted the water in a wide, white glistening path that hurt the eyes; and back where the horizon should be there was really none at all, there was only this pale blue, shimmering haze where sky and water merged without a discernible break. And the sea was even more remarkable: Roberts had never seen the sea quite like this. There wasn't a ripple anywhere; there was only the faintest hint of a ground swell, an occasional bulge of water. The surface, glazed as it was with moonlight, looked heavy, coated, enameled: it was that perfect. The ship slid through the water with an oily hiss, and the bow cut the fabric like a casual knife. At the stern, the wake was a wide, frothing rent, but farther back it was healing and not so wide, and far, far back the fabric was whole and perfect again.

Holy Christ, thought Roberts, this sea is a phony, a mirage, an illusion. There couldn't be a sea like this. It's a lie, a myth, a legend. It's not real.

And a not-at-all faint, interior voice answered him: Don't you wish it weren't?

Yes, said Roberts, I do for a fact: I wish it weren't.

And then he added: But this ship can't be real. There couldn't possibly be a ship like this.

The voice concurred: You're right there. There couldn't be.

But there is, Roberts said.

But there is, the voice agreed.

'Like a damn mill pond,' said a voice at his side; a more plausible and more corporeal voice. Roberts looked up at Dolan, the second-class quartermaster.

'The smoothest I ever saw it,' Roberts said.

'It really is.' Dolan looked about, almost squinting in the shiny moonlight. 'What a hell of a night to be out in this place!'

'I was thinking the same thing.'

Dolan, his eyes still scanning the water, shook his head. 'Man, that beats me.' He was young, only twenty-one or so, but he was a smart one; savvy; shrewd. He had been aboard not quite a year, and in that time he had established himself as one of the most formidable crapshooters on the ship. From his first day aboard, he had stood watches with Roberts, and a nice feeling had grown up between the two. When they stood a watch there wasn't any nicely shaded officer-enlisted-man relationship: there wasn't even any awareness of difference. They just stood and talked together: two men with the mutual background of the United States, the bond of this ship, a mutual dislike of the Captain; stood and gossiped and speculated and told stories and reminisced: things two men together are apt to do anywhere. Their watches were really one continued conversation which they could resume at any time with no consciousness of a break.

'Crap game tonight?' Roberts asked.

'Yeah,' Dolan said. 'I played till about eleven, then I quit.'

'How'd you make out?'

'Horseshit. That's why I quit. I couldn't hit a lick. I went in with a hundred and I dropped that and then I borrowed fifty from Vanessi and I came back a little, but then I dropped that too. So I figured it was time to get out of there.'

'Who won all the money?'

'Vanessi. Dowdy and him. That guy Vanessi was up about eight hundred bucks when I got out. He was hotter than a firecracker.'

Dolan was quiet a moment, then he said suddenly: 'By the way, did you hear about Dowdy? Him and the Old Man?'

'No. What did he do?'

Dolan laughed delightedly, an obviously choice morsel to present. 'That son-of-a-bitch, you know what he did? Tonight? The Old Man called him up, something about the boats, and when they got through the Old Man started crying the blues to Dowdy about the officers on here; what a miserable bunch of officers there was, and what a miserable outfit the Navy is, and how he wished he was back in the merchant service and could get hold of some of the officers back there. And then he says to Dowdy: "I know the officers on here hate my guts. That's all right; I don't care about that. Now tell me what the crew thinks of me." And Dowdy looks at him and says, "You really want to know, Captain?" And then he says: "Okay, you asked me and I'm telling you. Captain, they think you're a prick." '

'Hooray for Dowdy!' Roberts said. He clapped the pelorus. 'He really said that?'

'Absolutely! He said, "Captain, they think you're a prick." And he said the old man turned blue in the face, he was so mad; and at first he couldn't even talk, he was that mad. Then he told Dowdy to get the hell out of his cabin!'

'Say, that's wonderful!' Roberts said admiringly. 'I'm going to see to it that Dowdy gets recommended for the Navy Cross.'

The two worked on the Dowdy incident until its possibilities were exhausted; then they moved on to other matters. Dolan did most of the talking: he was a garrulous young man with impressively complete information on all strata of shipboard life, which he passed on faithfully to Mr. Roberts. Roberts, in turn, supplied opinion when asked, advice when asked, and a certain amount of information on officers' doings, which were somewhat inaccessible to Dolan's probing. Like all good gossip sessions, theirs was a reciprocal affair, and like a good session it served its purpose; it passed a weary hour. Tonight they each had another story of the Captain to offer, but, following on the perfect finality of the Dowdy incident, these sounded dull and anti-climactic. Then Dolan held forth for some time on the quality of the latest batch of jungle juice that Olson had brewed. Dolan's argument was that the beverage would be improved by sticking to straight raisin mash and omitting such miscellaneous and accidental fruit juices as could be stolen from the issue room. Roberts conceded he might be right. Then Dolan asked Roberts's opinion of the chances of getting sent back to the States with a fungus infection of the ear. This, in turn, led to a discussion of various ways of getting a medical survey which lasted for quite a while. When there was a lull in the talk, Dolan looked at his watch. 'Jeez, a quarter of two,' he said. 'Okay if I go down for some coffee?' Roberts said it was, although it always took Dolan half an hour to get a cup of coffee.

'Shall I bring you some?' Dolan said, starting down the ladder. Roberts shook his head.

Alone on the wing again, he took his glasses and studied the horizon. There was nothing there; there was nothing at all in the night but this ship, the point of reference in infinity, and this sea that planed away in all directions to the curving line of its visible limits. A little wind had come up, and on the sea there was a little swell; the ship rolled in it ever so gently and slowly. Roberts watched as the foremast wheeled in a stately arc against the stars of the Southern Cross, a pointer tracing on the blackboard of the sky. A quarter of two: well, that was good; that was better than he expected. That's where it paid to have someone to talk to, someone like Dolan; the time went down so much more easily. A quarter of two. Two hours down, two to go. It was when you were alone like this, nothing to do, no one to talk with, that the time went hard. It was a hundred times better to run in convoy and be busy as hell; a station to keep, the zigzag plan to run, ships to watch out for. It was when you were alone like this, no ships and no Dolan to engage the front of your mind, that it got bad. You started thinking then, and that was always bad. Never think: that was one of the two great lessons Roberts had learned. The other was, once started, how to stop thinking. When his mind started to work in the all-too-frequent pattern — subjectively, wishfully, unrealistically or too realistically and, in the end, despairingly — there was only one thing to do and that was to stop it; to wipe his mind blank as a slate washed with a sponge, and to keep it that way. He had learned to do that, and he considered the knowledge a priceless boon. He could stand for hours as he did now, his mind shuttered like a lens; and the tiny corner of it that would never quite close completely engrossed with such an external as the mast pirouetting among the stars, or the phosphorous that flared in the bow wave. And sooner or later the watches always ended — he had learned that too — they always ended.

There were footsteps on the ladder and Dolan was back. He busied himself for a moment in the wheelhouse, getting the two-o'clock readings; then he came out. He was eating an apple and he handed one to the officer.

'Clocks go back an hour tomorrow night,' Dolan said between bites. 'Not on our watch, though.'

'Midnight?' Roberts said.

'I guess so. Christ, they'd better. I think we've caught all the long watches so far. And then, when we go the other way and the clocks go ahead, we miss all of those. That's a bunch of crap!'

Dolan worked his apple down to the core and threw it over the side. 'What time does Frisco keep?' he asked suddenly.

'Frisco?' Roberts said. 'I think plus seven. Why?'

'Plus seven,' Dolan mused, 'plus seven. We're in minus eleven now. That's six hours' difference.' He ticked off on his fingers. 'Man, do you know what time it is in Frisco right now? It's eight o'clock!'

'That's right,' said Roberts. 'Eight o'clock yesterday.'

'Son-of-a-bitch!' Dolan was impressed. 'Think of that, Mr. Roberts. Eight o'clock. Just the time to be starting out in Frisco!'

Roberts didn't say anything and the quartermaster went on: 'Man, how I'd like to be down on Turck Street right now. Just going into the old Yardarm. Things would just be starting to pop down there! Were you ever in the Yardarm, Mr. Roberts?'

Roberts smiled. 'Once.'

'I knew it!' Dolan said. 'I might have known you'd get down there. It's all right, ain't it, the old Yardarm?'

'A little strenuous,' Roberts said.

'More beasts down there than you can shake a stick at!' Dolan was getting enthusiastic in his recollection. 'You know what, Mr. Roberts? The last time I was there, that was a year ago, man, I found a fine little beast. Cutest little doll you ever saw, blonde, a beautiful figure, really a beautiful girl. I was pretty stupid drunk, but I saw her and I started dancing with her and she started rubbing it up and boy, I sobered up in a hurry. I said, "Let's go someplace else, baby," and she said, "Let's go," and we went out the door and I said, "Where we going?" and she said, "Come with me." And we got in her car and she drove me right out to her apartment way out by U.C. Hospital. She had an apartment all to herself and this fine car, and, man, I was shacked up with her for a month. Her old man owned three bars and she was always getting me liquor and I was driving all over town in that Plymouth convertible and all the time shacked up with that fine beast. That was all right!'

Dolan shook his head wonderingly. He was all wound up now. He went on and on, recalling other conquests in San Francisco. Roberts listened for a while, but gradually his mind wandered. He nodded his head at the right places, and smiled at the right places, but he was no longer listening. Against his will, knowing he shouldn't be doing it, he was thinking of San Francisco; he was back there himself now, reconstructing his own version of the town. He was thinking of eight o'clock, the hour when the evening came to life; drawing upon his intensely maintained recollections of two and a half years ago. He was thinking of the signs lighting up along Geary Street, and the lineup waiting for taxis in front of the Saint Francis, and the cable cars climbing Nob Hill, and the dusk settling on Nob Hill, filling up from the bay and from the city below. Eight o'clock in the nice bars — the Saint Francis and the Cirque Room at the Fairmont and the Top of the Mark and the Zebra Room at the Huntington — the air bright and murmurous with the laughter and the clink of glasses and the foolish, confidential talk; and over it all, soft and unheard and really astonishingly sad, the deep, slow rhythms of American dance music.

And the girls, the fine, straight, clean-limbed American girls in their tailored suits, sitting, leaning forward, each talking with her escort, one hand extended on the table and just touching his sleeve. Or dancing tall and proud to the music that promised them bright and lovely and imperishable things. And at the bar all the young officers, the bright-eyed, expectant young officers, watching the girls, looking for something — they didn't know what — something that called at night with the dusk and the neon lights and swore to them that tonight, this very night, in this town, this bar, a thing of desperate loveliness would happen if only they found the right girl, found the right bar, drank enough liquor, smoked enough cigarettes, heard enough talk, laughed enough. But they must hurry, they must hurry! — the bars were closing, the ships were sailing, youth itself was running out. What was it they were seeking? It wasn't just a girl, although a girl was necessary. A girl wasn't the total; she was just a factor. It was more than that, Roberts thought — what was it?

And the angry, critical, voice inside him answered: Why, you goddamn knucklehead! Who're you trying to kid? The bars are so goddamn noisy you can't yell from one table to the next. The women are a bunch of beasts with dirty bare legs and stringy hair. The boys are out for just one thing and that's to get laid. Who're you trying to kid, anyway?

Dolan was asking him something. He wanted to know: 'Any chance of this bucket ever getting back to the States?'

Roberts said mildly. 'You know better than that.'

'Yeah,' Dolan said, 'I guess so. But the engineers keep saying we've got to get in a yard pretty soon.'

'And they've been saying that ever since I've been aboard. There's nothing wrong with these engines that can't be taken care of right out here.'

Dolan shook his head sadly. 'Yeah, this bucket will be running around here till the war's over.' He added determinedly: 'But this kid is sure as hell going to get back before then. As soon as I get eighteen months in, if they don't send me back then, whiz over the hill I go!'

Roberts turned and smiled. 'What are you going to do, swim?'

'If necessary!' Dolan said emphatically. 'If necessary! Do you know there are thousands of bastards lying around the States who've never been to sea? Yeoman and storekeepers and all that crap. Thousands of them!'

'That doesn't help us any.'

'No, but it should,' Dolan said. 'How long you been out of the States, Mr. Roberts?'

'How long? Oh, two and a half years. Thirty-three months exactly.'

'Jesus Christ!' Dolan said, impressed. 'That's a long time! How come?'

Roberts pinched his ear thoughtfully. 'I have a theory that all my records have blown out the window at the Bureau.'

'But thirty-three months! That's a *long* time!'

Yes, Roberts thought, it probably was a long time. He wasn't sure just how long, but it must have been quite long. He thought of his little sister for a greater comprehension of thirty-three months than the calendar provided. Thirty-three months had been long enough for his little sister, four years younger, to meet a man, fall in love with him, marry him, and bear a child for him. It was long enough for his sister who had been slim and blonde and pretty, to become, according to the evidence of the camera, no longer slim, no longer pretty, and more than thirty-three months older. It had been long enough, he wondered, for how many couples to fall in love and marry and have children, for how many pretty girls to lose their looks? If all the couples who had met and married within that period were to march four abreast past a given point, how long would the procession take? A hell of a long time, he decided; probably another two and a half years.

'I know one thing,' Dolan was saying, 'when I do get back I'm sure as hell going to get married. Little girl in Lakeland, Florida. Cute as hell. Did I ever show you her picture?'

Roberts shook his head and Dolan said: 'I got it right here.' He pulled a wallet out of his dungaree pants and in the ample moonlight they stood and examined the likeness of a round-eyed, gentle-looking girl with bobbed blond hair.

'Very pretty girl,' Roberts said.

'I'm going to marry that gal,' Dolan said. 'And then when I get out, I'm going to settle down right there in Lakeland and raise ferns. Make a million dollars growing ferns.'

'Ferns?'

'Hell, yeah. There's a lot of money in them. People just don't realize. You can make a lot of money growing ferns if you get a little good ground.'

'I didn't know,' Roberts said politely.

'Yeah, hell, yes,' Dolan said. 'What are you going to do when you get out?'

Roberts picked up a pair of glasses and raised them to his eyes. 'I haven't the faintest idea. Run a chain of whore-houses, maybe. Grow ferns. Sell apples. Any-thing.'

'What were you doing before you came in?'

Roberts looked through the glasses a moment with-out answering; then he put them down. 'I was going to school,' he said. 'Medical school. I'd just finished my first year.'

'Medical school? How come they got you in this outfit?'

'I came in. It was my own idea.'

'Yeah, but how come? The draft couldn't get you in medical school, could it?'

'No.'

'And you still joined this outfit?' Dolan insisted. 'When you didn't have to?'

Roberts smiled a crooked smile. 'That was right after Pearl Harbor. For some reason I felt I had to get in the war.' He shrugged as though to dismiss the subject. 'I don't understand it myself now.'

Dolan was not to be put aside. 'Jesus,' he said. 'I shouldn't think you would. If I had a chance like that to stay out, I sure as hell wouldn't be here now!'

'Jesus,' he said again; and after a moment: 'How many times a day do you kick yourself, Mr. Roberts?'

'Several hundred,' Roberts said quietly. 'An average of several hundred.'

'Are you going back to medical school when you get out?'

Roberts shook his head and squinted up at the foremast. 'Too old,' he said. 'I was twenty-two when I came in, I'm twenty-six now, I'll be twenty-eight when I get out. That's too old. I'd have to take a year of refresher work, then three more years of med school, then two years interning. That would make me thirty-four before I even started practicing. That's too much.'

The quartermaster was quiet a moment. 'Jesus,' he said after a moment, softly, 'why in the *hell* did you want to get in the war?'

Roberts's answer wasn't really an answer at all. 'I didn't know then that there were such things as auxiliaries,' he mused. 'I just took for granted that I'd get on a can or a wagon or a carrier right in the middle of it. Instead I end up on a tanker in the Atlantic and this thing out here.'

'Jesus,' Dolan said again. He shook his head doubtfully and looked at his wrist. 'Three o'clock,' he announced, 'five after.' He went into the wheelhouse to get the readings. He came back and leaned on the pelorus and the two stood together and looked out at the sea. A minute passed, and another, and then the watch collapsed, fell apart, was finished, done with. One minute it was three o'clock, and the next it was four. One minute Dolan was telling a story about the girl friend of Dowdy's who got her picture in *True Detective* for shooting her husband, and the next it was three-thirty and time to call the reliefs. And from three-thirty, with no interval at all, the clock jumped to a quarter of four and Dolan was making an informal salute and spieling all in one breath and almost in one word, 'I've been relieved sir Garrity has the watch,' and there was Ed Pauley standing beside him, rubbing his eyes and yawning.

'A hell of a time to get a man up,' Pauley mumbled.

And the watch was over. 'It is that, Ed,' Roberts said quietly. 'It is that.'

Pauley scowled around the horizon. 'What's the dope?'

'Two-five-eight. Seventy-two turns. No course changes. No zigzag. Stupid has a call in for six.'

Pauley nodded. 'I saw that. Okay,' he said. 'I got it.'

'Okay,' said Roberts. He turned to go.

'Say,' called Pauley. 'Have you got *God's Little Acre?*'

'No, I don't have it. Keith had it the last time I saw it.'

'He's too young to be reading that,' Pauley pronounced soberly.

'That's true.' Roberts went on into the charthouse and wrote his log. When he had finished, he sat for a moment slumped on the stool at the chart-table, rubbing his eyes. He considered going down to the wardroom for something to eat, then he remembered there was nothing there. He got up slowly and went down the ladder to his room.

Nothing had changed: it could have been seconds .

that he had been gone. Langston was still breathing with the same rhythm and the same intensity. With the same whine the fan was pushing the same air across the room. The clock ticked on and on. Roberts undressed in the dark and got into bed. He lay on his back, his arms cradled beneath his head, his eyes open and staring into the darkness. Helplessly, before he could stop himself, he thought again of San Francisco. Now, as he saw it, it was midnight there and the bars were letting out; the couples walked arm in arm down the streets and the women laughed, and all of them were rich with the knowledge of some incomparable party to follow. A boy and a lovely, slender girl with shining black hair came out of the Mark and stepped into a taxicab, and as the taxi pulled away the girl lay back in the seat and turned to the boy with a slow, happy, secret smile. And down the steep face of the California street, past the careless, oblivious couples, a young man walked alone; back to the ship, the camp, the empty hotel room; another night spent of the dwindling supply, and nothing bought. What was he looking for? What was he missing? What had he lost?

And then the sudden, angry voice clamored: Will you knock it off? Will you for Christ's sake knock it off?

Abruptly as turning out a light Roberts stopped thinking, shut off his mind, composed himself for sleep. Mechanically, through the tiny corner left open, he calculated the day ahead: four hours of sleep now, the four to eight watch in the afternoon, and then all night in — no watch until eight the next morning. A whole night in — that was something to look forward to.

To A SUPERFICIAL OBSERVER, it might seem that there was a minimum of high, clear purpose to Ensign Pulver's life. A very close observer, scrutinizing Pulver under the lens, would reach the same conclusion. But if Pulver's direction was sometimes dubious, one thing

was abundantly certain — that he would travel it in considerable contentment. Ensign Pulver was a quite
happy and relaxed young man. He slept a great deal
and very well, ate practically anything without com-
plaint; and to any stimuli his reaction was apt to be
remarkably amiable. He could and did absorb stagger-
ing amounts of well-intentioned insult, and his vanity
appeared to be vulnerable on only one point: his feet.
By accepted human standards, Ensign Pulver's feet
were enormous, and he was delicate about them. He
was apt to become abruptly dignified and not a little
aloof when they were offered for discussion. They were
offered frequently.

Ensign Pulver was a young man of a high degree of
ingenuity. Most of this he directed toward his own
well-being. Since foresight is the better part of ingenuity, he had reported aboard the ship burdened
with a large and heavy wooden box. It would be
fatuous to presume that this chest contained clothing.
The three cases of beer, six quarts of bourbon, three of
rum, one of gin, and two of Vermouth, had lasted,
through admirable providence, almost six months, even
though shared with Lieutenant Roberts and Ed Pauley
and the Doc. Pulver had himself, over the objections of
the other three, imposed the pace and the restraint. He
had a predilection for certain things effete and sen-
suous, and he got a wonderful feeling of luxury from
lying in his bunk sipping a beer or a Manhattan.

Young Pulver got to spending a lot of time in his
bunk, asleep and awake. On an average day he prob-

ably spent eighteen hours in bed. He was an engineering officer. Although few of the officers had anything,
really, to do, Pulver had less than most. It would be
neither unfair nor very inaccurate to say that, profes-
sionally, he didn't do a thing. So he had a lot of time
on his hands, and this, with his native ingenuity, he
converted to time on his back. His bunk became to him
a sort of shrine, and but for meals and other undeniable
functions, he was seldom out of it. It was an unusually
well-equipped bunk. At the foot Pulver had rigged a
small fan which wafted cool breezes over him on the hot-
test nights. At the side was attached a coffee-can ash
tray, a container for cigarettes and another for a lighter.
Pulver liked to smoke in bed while he was reading. Books
were stowed in the space between the springs and the
bulkhead. Beer was kept there, too, and it was possible
to open a bottle on the reading light on the bulkhead.

He read a great deal, being embarked upon an am-
bitious program of self-improvement. By education
Pulver was a metallurgical engineer, and now read
books that he had widely and willingly evaded during
his college days. He read these books because they
were the books that Lieutenant Roberts read; consciously or not, Ensign Pulver had set out to make himself over in Roberts's image. With regard to most
objects, people, ideas, Pulver was languidly cynical;
with a few he was languidly approving, and with almost
none was he overtly enthusiastic. His admiration for
Roberts was utterly unabashed. He thought that Roberts was the greatest guy he had ever known. He

prodded him with questions on every conceivable subject, memorized the answers, then went back to his bunk and assiduously absorbed them into his own conversation. He watched the careless, easy dignity with which Roberts met the crew, and studied the way that Roberts got the crew to work for him; and then he tried to apply this dignity and this control to his own small authority. Being honest with himself, he couldn't notice any increased devotion in the eyes of the men; or indeed, anything more than the usual tolerance. It is not very likely that Ensign Pulver would ever have read Santayana, or the English philosophers, or *Jean Christophe*, or *The Magic Mountain*, if he had not seen Roberts reading them. Before this self-imposed apprenticeship, he had been content to stay within the philosophical implications of *God's Little Acre*. He had read *God's Little Acre* twelve times, and there were certain passages he could recite flawlessly.

His reading program didn't leave much time for anything else, but what leisure could be managed he devoted to planning characteristically ingenious actions against the Captain. He didn't really have cause for hard feeling against the Captain, because, being an engineer, he was quite remote from him. In truth, the Captain hardly knew Pulver was aboard. But because Roberts hated the Captain, Pulver felt duty-bound to do the same; and scarcely a day went by that he didn't present to Roberts the completed planning for a new offensive. To be sure, these offensives seldom went beyond the planning stage, because commonly their structure was so satisfying to Ensign Pulver that he felt fulfilled just in regarding it. Also he was not a very brave young man, and these things called for bravery just as surely as the battlefield.

Once he figured out a way to plug, far down in the sanitary system, the line that fed the Captain's head, so that the Captain would one day be deluged by a considerable backwash. He never did anything about it. He figured out a Rube Goldberg device that would punch the Captain in the face with a gloved fist when he entered his cabin. He never did anything about this either. Then he was going to introduce marbles into the overhead in the Captain's bedroom, the marbles to roll around at night and make an awful racket. He conferred frequently with the Doctor on ways of transmitting a gonococcus infection to the Captain. About the only plan he ever executed was one involving no personal risk. He did, one day while the Captain was ashore, actually insert shavings from an electric razor into his bed, on the theory that they would serve as satisfactorily as any good itch powder. If they did, the evidences were disappointing, for although Pulver watched closely, the Captain never appeared better-rested, and indeed, better-natured, than in the succeeding days.

One day, during a lull in his reading schedule, a wonderful idea for the Captain came to Pulver. It was one so stunning that he was able to recognize it immediately as his *tour de force*. It did not reveal itself to him gradually, as did most of his schemes, but instead it came with the sudden, inevitable force of predestination. It was, quite simply, tremendous: he would get some good substantial firecrackers and throw them into the Old Man's room at night. It was a wonderful idea, and yet it was so simple, so indicated, and so necessary, that Pulver marveled he hadn't thought of it before. The bastard would be walking on his heels for weeks afterward! What a splendid idea! Ensign Pulver dedicated several full minutes to self-gratulation.

After the first flush of creation, he permitted himself a little to be invaded by realism. He owned no firecrackers, he was sure there were none on the ship, and it was likely that the closest supply was at Honolulu, distant about two thousand miles. But such second-rate obstacles were no match for a thing predestined, and he easily surmounted them. Fireworks, he decided strongly, could be manufactured on the ship. Black powder, he thought, would do very nicely. He could make some kind of a fuse too. The idea was a natural — it couldn't possibly fail.

When the plan was complete and glowing in his mind, he took it, as he took all of his plans, to Lieutenant Roberts. This was quite late at night and Roberts had turned in. He wasn't very enthusiastic when he was awakened to hear the new plan: in fact, he was definitely hostile, if not to the plan, then at least to Pulver. He cursed Pulver vigorously. Then he turned over and went back to sleep.

Ensign Pulver was a little hurt at this reception, but it didn't diminish his faith in the plan one whit. He lay in his bunk that night and stayed awake an excessively long time, fifteen minutes or so, savoring the whole thing. The more he thought about it, the better it seemed. He went over in his mind just how it would be. He debated deliciously whether to attach a long time-fuse to the explosive, or to fix a short one, light it, throw it, and run like hell. He finally decided in favor of the short fuse as being the more exciting. He fell happily asleep, mesmerized by a vision of Captain Morton, pop-eyed with terror, quaking at the explosions that rocked his very sanity.

Next morning he was up at the unprecedented hour of nine. He went right to work. He found some good stout twine to use as a fuse. For a container he cut into firecracker lengths the cardboard roll of a clothes-hanger. He went down to sick-bay and begged some potassium sulphate to saturate the fuse. Then he was ready for the explosive. Ensign Pulver was a competent metallurgist, but his knowledge of explosives was deficient. He had, in the course of the night, abandoned black powder as his choice and substituted fulminate of mercury. He knew that by repute fulminate of mercury was terrific stuff, and he reasoned that the best was none too good for this job. He went down to Olson, the gunner's mate, and obtained four primers used to detonate the old model five-inch bag ammunition. The primers contained fulminate of mercury.

He was ready then for the test. In a state of high excitement he hurried down to the machine shop just aft of the engine room. The place was well chosen for its subterranean location, large cleared area, and corrugated steel deck. Ensign Pulver cut open the primers, sealed one end of a section of the cardboard tubing, filled the case with fulminate of mercury, inserted the potassium sulphate fuse and plugged the other end around it. He stood back then and viewed the product with an artist's pride. It bulged ominously and did not much resemble a firecracker. Ensign Pulver hummed and smiled happily as he found a match and lit the one-inch fuse.

He had made two miscalculations. They were fairly grave. He had underestimated the rate at which the potassium sulphate fuse would burn. It went like a streak. And he had grossly underestimated and completely misunderstood the explosive character of fulminate of mercury, which, particle for particle, is just about the most furious substance in the world. The signalmen, way up on the flying bridge, claimed that they could feel the explosion; and certainly every man on the ship heard it. The men in the engine room were terrified; they knew that finally a torpedo had struck. If the Captain had been aboard, he would almost certainly have been screaming, 'Prepare to abandon ship!' It was quite a firecracker.

The Doc said that Ensign Pulver got off very light. His eyebrows and lashes were burned off, and the hair for an area of two inches back from his forehead. He received first-degree burns of the face, neck, and forearms. He was in sick-bay for a day soaking in tannic acid. After that he was up and around, but with his head and throat swathed like a mummy. Perhaps he was a proper object for sympathy, but his appearance short-circuited any that might have been forthcoming. He looked pretty silly without eyebrows and with his nose sticking out from the bandages like a beacon.

Just as a matter of policy Ensign Pulver always tried to avoid the Captain. He did pretty well, too, sometimes going two and three weeks without even seeing him. Now, however, just a few days after his accident, rounding a corner in the boat-deck passageway, he ran smack into Captain Morton. The Captain hadn't seen or heard of Pulver's condition, and his response was typically childlike. For a moment he gaped and goggled, and then he started chuckling. He had a particularly lewd and rasping chuckle, and he stood pointing at the turbaned Pulver and laughing like a child confronted by a clown.

'What the hell'd you do?' he demanded. 'Stick your head in one of them goddam furnaces down there?' And he chuckled the more at his own wit.

Ensign Pulver forced a grin, said 'Yessir,' and started edging toward the down ladder.

The Captain looked at him benevolently. 'Goddamn, boy,' he chortled, 'you want to keep your head out of those furnaces. Don't you know that?'

Pulver made another grin, said 'Yessir' again sheepishly, and then, when he saw a chance only moderately rude, he ducked down the ladder. He was so furious he couldn't see straight. The goddamned smart-aleck, loud-mouthed son-of-a-bitch! He tried very hard to keep his anger focused on the Captain, but all the time he knew better. What really rubbed, he knew, was his conviction of the considerable justice in the Captain's laughter.

LIEUTENANT CARNEY, the first division officer, and Lieutenant (jg) Billings, the communicator, had a fight one day. It wasn't a fight, really — more of a spat than anything else — but even so aborted a difference between the two was an event of genuineness. Until this

particular day they had roomed together for fifteen
months without so much as a sharp word. While the
other officers fretted and cursed and complained,
Carney and Billings had made a separate peace with
each other and with the ship. While the other officers
prowled the ship and plotted against the Captain and
wore themselves out seeking diversion, these two lay in
their bunks and wrestled such conflicts as whether to
get up now or wait half an hour until noon. Carney
and Billings had reduced life in stateroom number nine
to the ultimate simplicity, and were working constantly
to push it beyond that point. All the needs of man
were right there: the room owned a private head and
twenty steps down the passageway was the wardroom
with its food and coffee Silex and acey-deucey board.
What more could a man want? Billings hadn't been
out of the amidships house in two months, since the
time he got lost looking for the paint locker.

They lived a little idyll in stateroom number nine.
Billings, who stood no watches, slept every day until
noon, but one day out of four Carney had to get up at
eight. The process of arising at noon and greeting the
not-very-new day was always the same: Billings, who
occupied the top bunk, would dangle an arm or a leg
over the side; Carney would command fiercely, 'Get
back in there where you belong'; Billings would comply
and say meekly: 'I'm sorry'; and Carney would finish
off, 'And stay there!' This happened three days out of
four, and every day — sometimes two and three times a
day — another little ritual would be acted out. One

would say to the other: 'Feel like getting your ass
whipped?'; to which the reply was: 'Think you're man
enough?': and the reply to that was: 'Yes, I think so.'
Then the two would march to the wardroom, for this
was the invitation to acey-deucey combat.

These sequences were the fixed points of the day, the
clichés, the rituals, and like all rituals they were performed automatically, unconsciously, and without
awareness of repetition. The plan for the rest of the
day was fixed too, but it allowed some small room for
improvisation. There were at least two ways in which
the afternoon could be spent. Carney was from
Osceola, Iowa, where he operated his father's shoe
store; Billings was from Minnesota, where he ran a
dairy farm. Many afternoons slipped by in thoughtful
talk, Carney picturing for Billings the romance of the
shoe business, Billings pointing out the grievously neglected fascination of animal husbandry. Other happy
afternoons would be devoted to what might be called
(if the word did not imply the contrasting present of a
gainful occupation) avocations. Carney painted in
water colors. He started out on landscapes: he painted
a simple pastoral scene, animals grazing in a field, but
perspective gave him unexpected trouble, and the cows
seemed to be suspended in air over the pigs. He decided he wasn't ready for landscapes. Next he did from
a photograph a portrait of his wife, but it was un-
fortunate too. One eye was larger than the other and
focused in another direction, the nose was crooked
and the mouth was pulled up as though with paralysis.

Carney decided he wasn't ready for portraits either, and painted from life a red and yellow-striped thermos bottle which was more successful.

Billings's hobby was socialism. He had acquired it unexpectedly by reading Upton Sinclair, and been confirmed in it by the pamphlets of Norman Thomas and the essays of Bertrand Russell. He had placed himself on the mailing list of twelve Socialist organs and three Communist, and these of an afternoon he would read aloud to Carney at his painting. Billings tried earnestly to bring Carney to his persuasion, but, although Carney always listened politely, it was clear that he would not become a convert during Billings's lifetime. In the room, though, they lived a quite definite communal life. When the laundry was late, Carney wore Billings's scivvies, and Billings Carney's shirts. Whichever toothpaste happened to be out was the one used. Books had no ownership at all. Through an unuttered agreement Billings supplied cigarettes and soap for the room, while Carney provided Coca-Cola, which he had bought from a merchant ship. Everything in stateroom nine was organized like that; every problem that life could throw up was absorbed, smothered, controlled. Carney and Billings had made an approach to Nirvana equaled by few in our time. It was strange, then, that they should have this quarrel.

It happened while the ship was unloading again at Apathy island. It was a wretched place, flat and rank and bilious green; bad enough to look at and worse to smell. Great fat swollen flies with a sting like a bee's swarmed out from the island and infested the ship. Long, vicious mosquitoes came out too. Eight- and ten-foot sharks patrolled the ship to prevent swimming. There wasn't a thing over on the beach; not an officers' club, not even a single bottle of beer. And hot! — all day long the sun pounded down through the breathless air, and all day the porous jungle absorbed and stored the heat. And then at night, when the sun had set and the cool time should begin, the jungle exhaled in a foul, steaming breath the day's accumulation of heated air. It was a maddening place; everyone got on the nerves of everyone else; there were five fist-fights while the ship was there. Still, you had a right to expect Carney and Billings to be impervious to all this.

The quarrel began in the morning and gathered momentum through the day. It began when it became too hot even to sleep, when both Carney and Billings awoke at the unheard-of hour of nine. For a while they lay in their bunks and didn't move and didn't talk. From the top bunk Billings could look out the porthole and see the glaring water and the seedy island. Carney couldn't see them from the bottom bunk, but he knew they were there. Then Billings dangled a foot over the edge of the bunk. 'Get back in there,' Carney said listlessly, out of old habit. Billings's answer was unexpected and startling: 'Cut it out,' he said sharply.

For a moment, after it was said, it was very quiet in there. Neither said any more and after a little Billings sat up and crawled down from his bunk. He was sweating and he plodded to the head to take a shower.

He came out cursing: the water was off: it was outside of water hours. Angrily, he put on his shoes and started dressing. He couldn't find his shirt right away. 'Where's my goddamn shirt?' he grumbled, more to himself than to Carney. It didn't require an answer, but Carney, smarting under Billings's testiness of a few minutes back, gave him one. 'How the hell should I know?' he snapped.

If Billings had said something then, if perhaps they had exchanged a few words, they might have removed the whole matter from their chests. But Billings turned his back and didn't say a word. He went down to the wardroom for a cup of coffee and he was sore. He was sore and simmering when he went into the wardroom, but when there was no coffee on the Silex he flared into anger. That son-of-a-bitch, he thought: and curiously enough he wasn't designating the steward's mate who had neglected the coffee, he was thinking of Carney.

Within the next half-hour a combination of several things set his nasty temper like plaster. Upon investigation he found that tonight's movie was a dreary, stupid musical which had already been shown once on the ship and which he had seen in the States three years ago. That took the last bit of hope from the day right there. Then the Captain called him up and ate his ass out for the way the signalmen were keeping the flying bridge. After that Billings sat down and broke a message which ordered the ship, upon completing discharge, right back to the place it had left, a place almost as sorry as this. And, finally, he learned that the unloading was going very slowly, so slowly that they wouldn't be out of here for a week anyway. Everyone had counted on getting out in four days at the most.

That did it, the last piece of news did it. A little later Billings went down to the room. Carney was up now, sitting at the desk in his shorts writing a letter. His clothes were thrown across Billings's bunk. Billings exploded: 'Get your goddamn crap off my bed!' He flung the clothes onto the bottom bunk.

Carney didn't look up from his letter. 'Screw you, you silly bastard,' he said coldly.

'Right through the nose,' Billings replied and went out. The thing was declared then; it was out in the open. From then on, it mounted steadily. Noon chow, consisting of a New England boiled dinner despised by all, eaten in collaboration with a hundred arrogant flies, didn't help matters. After lunch Carney got into the room first and into the shower first. That was at twelve-thirty; the water went off promptly at one. Billings wanted very much to take a shower. He sat around the room quite obviously waiting to do so. At one minute to one Carney, singing happily, stepped out of the shower.

'You're pretty goddamn smart, aren't you?' Billings snarled.

'I think so,' said Carney blandly.

'Jesus!' Billings said disgustedly. He stalked out and the heat of his anger climbed higher and higher. 'Jesus, he fumed, what a cheap son-of-a-bitch!' As the afternoon wore on, he thought furiously and obsessionally of his roommate, and the more he thought, the angrier he got. And, curiously, the angrier he got, the thirstier he got. By three o'clock he craved a drink, specifically a Coca-Cola, more than anything in the world. Every afternoon at three he and Carney would drink a Coca-Cola cooled with ice from the wardroom refrigerator. It had become an addiction for both, and Billings had to have his now. It was, of course, out of the question to ask that son-of-a-bitch Carney for one, so Billings decided to steal it. But when he went down to the room to accomplish this, Carney was there, sitting at the desk, approximately the size of life. He was painting what seemed to be a native outrigger canoe, and on the desk beside him was a frosty glass of Coca-Cola. Billings went out without a word. Craftily he went to the wardroom and seated himself so that he could watch the door. It wasn't long until Carney came out and went down the passageway. It wasn't long then until Billings streaked for the room. The cokes, he well knew, were at the bottom of Carney's closet. He was delighted with himself, exhilaratingly revenged, elated, until he tried the closet door. It was locked.

To Billings's credit, it must be said that he took this in stride. He did the only thing possible under the circumstances. He collected all of the cigarettes, all the matches, all the soap, even tiny slivers from the trays, and locked them in his drawer. It wasn't enough, but it was the only thing he could do. He went out and when it was time to wash up for evening chow, he returned to the room. Carney was still there. Without a word Billings unlocked his drawer, took out the soap and washed himself. Then he locked up the soap again.

Carney watched, smiling superiorly. 'My,' he said, 'aren't we smart?'

'I think so,' said Billings. He knew that Carney was burned up.

That was the penultimate round. The climax came after the movie. The picture turned out poor as everyone knew, and some of the crew didn't even wait for the finish. Billings and the amiable Ensign Pulver left early and were sitting talking in stateroom nine when Carney came in. Pulver, who was ignorant of the day's tension, greeted Carney cheerily: 'Hi, Louie,' he said. 'Sit down and let's have one of your cokes.'

Carney replied with a geniality that sharply excluded Billings. 'Frank,' he said, 'I think that's a fine idea. Let's you and I have one.'

Pulver thought it was some kind of game. 'Ain't you going to give old Alfy here one?' he said thoughtlessly.

Carney snorted. 'Hell, no! Let the son-of-a-bitch buy his own!'

Billings said immediately: 'Who the hell wants your cokes, you silly bastard?'

'Who wants them?' Carney said sweetly. 'You do. You'd give your left leg for a coke right now.'

'The hell I would.' Billings turned to Pulver, who was sitting very much surprised at this sharp and sincere exchange. He had never known the two to talk like this. 'Jesus,' said Billings scornfully, 'did you ever hear such a petty son-of-a-bitch? He's got his cokes locked up in that closet! Afraid somebody's going to get one of them!'

'I'm not afraid *you're* going to get any,' Carney sneered. 'That's for sure.'

Billings continued to address the bewildered Pulver. 'That is the cheapest son-of-a-bitch I ever knew. You could count on your fingers all the money he's spent since he's been on this ship. Mooch! — all the bastard does is mooch. He hasn't bought a cigarette since he's been on here. He's the penny-pinchingest, mooching-est bastard I ever knew!'

'Wouldn't you like a coke?' Carney taunted, but his face by this time was flushed red.

'Jesus, what an ass!' Billings was saying. 'What a petty no-good bastard! Sits on his ass all day and does these stupid paintings. Have you ever seen any of his paintings? — a five-year-old moron could do better!'

Carney couldn't keep the anger out of his voice now. 'Look who's talking! The sack-king himself! That son-of-a-bitch spends so much time in there he gets sores on his back. Actually!' He turned to Billings. 'Why don't you get up in your sack where you belong?' he sneered.

'Why don't you put me there?'

'I think that's a good idea!'

'I'd like to see it!'

It was a bad moment. Both roommates were on their feet ready to swing. Ensign Pulver, normally a rather ineffective young man, suddenly arose to greatness. He got between them and he made it a joke. 'Boys, boys, boys,' he soothed. 'Take it easy or Stupid'll be running down here.' He pushed Carney down in the chair and then he got Billings to sit down again on the bunk. For a moment they sat glowering at each other. Then Carney picked up the quarrel.

'Talk about petty,' he said to Pulver. 'Do you know what that guy did today? Actually did? He locked up little tiny slivers of soap so I couldn't use them! So small you could hardly see them, and he locked them up!' Carney shook his head. 'Boy, that beats me.'

'Nothing beats you,' Billings shot back, 'when it comes to pettiness. You're the world's champ!'

'And not only that,' Carney went on to Pulver, 'but the other day he was up banging ears with the Old Man again. He tells us he hates him and every chance he gets he sneaks up there and bangs ears. That's a nice guy to have around!'

'You wish you could get up there yourself, don't you, you son-of-a-bitch!'

Carney swung around in the chair. 'Better watch your language,' he said tightly.

'Why should I?' Billings challenged. 'Can you tell me why?'

Pulver stepped into the breach again. 'All right, god-damit,' he said sternly. 'Knock it off. It's too hot for such crap. Now knock it off, both of you.' Pulver probably surprised himself, but he was certainly effective.

Billings stood up and stretched elaborately. 'Yeah,' he said, 'you're right, Frank. It's getting boring in here. Let's you and I get out.'

'That's a fine idea,' said Carney. 'Not you, Frank,' he added.

Billings ignored this. 'Yeah, let's go visit our friends,' he said. 'The company's getting stupid in here.' He threw an arm around Pulver and led him toward the door.

'Yeah, go visit your friends,' Carney sneered. 'Billings has so many of them.'

Billings nodded knowingly to Pulver. 'Come on,' he said. Pulver hesitated in the doorway, obviously glad enough of an excuse to get out. 'I'll see you later, Louie,' he said impartially to Carney. Then he and Billings went out.

That was all, then; the thing was over. Billings sat for three hours with Pulver in the wardroom playing acey-deucey, and he lost every game but two. Ordinarily Pulver couldn't take a game from him, but to-night Billings was so gorged with anger that he couldn't see straight. His mind wasn't on the game, his mind was trying to figure some way to get at Carney, but he couldn't think of a thing. Finally at midnight they quit. Billings went in to go to bed. The room was dark, and Carney was already in bed. So, in the process of undressing, Billings turned all the lights on and slammed the door to the head as loudly as he could. Then he climbed into his bunk. He was just about asleep when all the lights flashed on and the head door slammed like an explosion. It was Carney retaliating.

That night it rained, and all night long it rained. Next morning it was still raining, a chill, shifting, con-

tinuous tropical rain. Both Carney and Billings awoke
at eight, felt the rain, pulled a sheet about them, and
went snugly back to sleep. At eleven, in co-ordination,
they awoke again, and both felt fine. A lovely cool
breeze was coming in the porthole, and outside the
rain was smoking on the water, so dense that Billings,
looking out, couldn't even see the hated island. He
yawned, stretched happily, and carelessly dropped an
arm over the side of the bunk. Before he remembered
and caught himself, Carney almost told him to get back
in there. After a while Billings got up and dressed.
'Jesus,' he said, 'rain.' He said it with just the right im-
personal inflection, that didn't necessarily invite a reply.
'Yeah,' said Carney. He said it just right, too; not too
coldly, not too cordially; just right. That was all the
conversation until noon.

All the officers were in good spirits at lunch. The rain
made them feel good, and besides, there was the news
that an extra stevedore gang was being assigned the
ship, which meant they'd be out of here in four days
after all. Not only that, but there was a good movie —
Rita Hayworth — scheduled for tonight, and it was only
six months old.

Billings felt so good that he went up to the radio
shack and did some work. As he worked, his glow of
general and diffused mellowness concentrated itself
into a beam of good feeling directed at Carney. He
thought what a good roommate Carney was. He
thought over the events of the previous day and how
foolish, really, the quarrel had been. He resolved to go
down and start patching things up.

In the room Carney was painting at the desk again. Billings went over to the washbasin and scrubbed his hands and scrupulously examined his teeth. Then, as he started out the door he said informatively, casually, and as though it had just occurred to him: 'Oh, say, the exec was looking for you.' Carney looked up and said politely: 'Yeah, thanks, I saw him.' Billings went back to the shack then and finished his work. He felt that they were ready now for a full reconciliation. It was about three o'clock, Coca-Cola time, when he returned to the room.

He stood peering attentively over Carney's shoulder. The work in progress was that of a red stone building of an architecture possible only for a courthouse or a schoolhouse, set in the center of a public square. The square had a lawn of bluish tint, and there were several improbable-looking trees scattered about. Atop the building was what was evidently intended for a cupola, but with its upcurved corners looked more like a pagoda.

'Where is that?' Billings asked respectfully.

Carney looked up and smiled. 'That's Osceola,' he said. 'The courthouse at Osceola, the county seat of Clark County.'

Billings continued to study the picture seriously. 'What's that?' he said, pointing to the pagoda-like structure.

'That's the cupola,' Carney said. He cocked his head at the picture and grinned. 'Those curves represent the Chinese influence on my work.'

Billings stroked his chin and with a perfectly dead-pan face he asked: 'Are you sure they don't represent the Asiatic influence?'

And then both of them were laughing easily together, and Carney, still laughing, was waving his hand and saying carelessly: 'Get the ice.'

Over the cokes, they sat back and examined the work critically. 'I think it's my best work,' Carney said. 'What do you think?'

'I think it is,' Billings agreed. He turned his head this way and that. 'You're getting good on sidewalks,' he noted.

'Yeah,' said Carney. 'I'm good on sidewalks. Those are pretty good trees, too, don't you think?'

Billings nodded. 'Fine trees,' he said positively.

They finished the cokes and Carney leaned back in his chair and yawned and stretched. 'Well,' he said. 'I've done enough work for today. I think I'll knock off.'

Billings yawned and stretched, too. He scratched his head. Very casually he said: 'Feel like getting your ass whipped?'

Carney cocked an eyebrow at him. 'Think you're man enough?'

'I think so,' Billings said.

'Okay.' They stood up and Carney led the way to the wardroom.

T HE ANCHORING ITSELF was accomplished without incident. The anchor chain banged and rattled in the hawse pipes and the ship shuddered as it stampeded out. The word, 'Secure the special sea detail,' was blatted over the P.A. system and five seconds later the engine room called the bridge for permission to secure the main engines. The Captain made the appropriate reply, 'Goddamit, they'll secure when I get good and ready to let them secure,' but he did it without enthusiasm, and he only muttered for perhaps two minutes about those bastards down there who sit on their tails waiting to secure. It was a very hot, sweaty day, about three in the afternoon, and it seemed just another island: so nobody's heart beat very much faster at being anchored.

The port routine commenced, a matter of loosening the ship's belt a notch or two. The gun watches stayed on, but the lookouts were secured and ran below to find the crap game. A boat was lowered to go over and get the mail. Back on number four hatch the canvas screen was rigged for the night's movie. Stuyzuiski, a seaman in the third division who wouldn't get out of his clothes under way, took a bath; and at chow everyone remarked on how much better he smelled. Ensign Pulver mixed himself what he called a Manhattan — a third of a water-glass of brandy, a splash of vermouth, and a couple of ice cubes — and lay in his bunk and sipped it admiringly. The crew leaned on the rail and looked around incuriously at the little bay and the naval base ashore. Becker, a seaman received on board in the last draft, was moved to remark to Dowdy: 'This ain't a bad place, you know it?' Dowdy said something obscene without even turning his head. Becker bumbled on: 'No, I mean it ain't as bad as most of the places we been to. It's kind of pretty.'

Becker was right, though; it *was* kind of pretty; **it was** really a rather lovely little bay. The water off the reef was terribly blue, a showy light-ink blue. The bay was enclosed by a chain of islands, and instead of the usual flat barren coral these were green with lush and heavy foliage, and on two sides of the anchorage they ran up to impressive hills that were remote and pur- pling in the late afternoon sun. And the channel at the end of the bay wound away into the deep shadow be- tween the islands and reappeared flashing in the secret and smoky distance. The crew, lined along the rail, began to feel obscurely good at being here; and even Dowdy was probably aware that, aesthetically, this was quite a superior place.

Its intrinsic and most spectacular virtue fell to Sam Insigna to discover. (Although if Sam hadn't found it one of the other signalman would have soon enough.) Sam was a little monkey of a man, not quite five feet tall, long-armed and bow-legged like a monkey, with a monkey's grinning, wizened face, who had achieved considerable fame aboard the ship by once attacking, unprovoked and with the intention of doing physical violence, a six-foot-four-inch marine. Sam was up on the flying bridge with the other signalmen and he was idly scanning the beach through the ship's telescope, a large, mounted glass of thirty-two power. The ship was anchored perhaps two hundred yards from the beach, and just off the starboard bow, the way she was head- ing now, there was a base hospital. The hospital flag was flying over three rows of Quonset huts; there was well-trimmed grass between the huts, and straight neat coral paths that looked like sidewalks. Farther off to the right was the rest of the naval base; clapboard buildings and Quonsets scattered between coconut palms, and down at the waterfront there was a long wooden dock where a Liberty ship was unloading. Dead ahead, right on the point, was the interesting thing, though, the really amazing thing. It was a house, easily identifiable as a house; an authentic civilian house. It was a wooden, two-story house, painted yellow; long and low, with a veranda running the entire length. There was a swing on the veranda and several cane chairs, there was a fine green lawn running down to the beach, and there were two green wooden benches on the lawn under the trees. It was an old house, obviously long antedating American occupation of the island; it was a formless, bleak, and even ugly house; yet, in these surroundings, in the middle of the Pacific, it seemed to the signalmen a thing of great magnificence.

'It must have been the Governor's house,' Schlemmer explained.

Sam swung the telescope around to have a look at this. At first he trained it carelessly around the grounds, then he turned it on the house. For perhaps a full minute nothing happened, and then it did. Sam had been leaning with one elbow on the windshield; all of a sudden he jerked upright, sucked in his breath and grabbed at the glass as if he were falling. The idea flashed through the mind of Schlemmer, standing beside him, that Sam had been hit by a sniper.

'Holy Christ!' Sam said. He seemed to have difficulty in speaking.

'What is it?' Schlemmer said, and he grabbed for a long-glass.

There was only reverence in Sam's voice. 'Holy Christ! She's bare-assed!'

One of the many anomalies of our ponderous Navy is its ability to move fast, to strike the swift, telling blow at the precise moment it is needed. There were accessible in the wheelhouse and charthouse seven pairs of binoculars; on the flying bridge were two spyglasses and two long-glasses, and the ship's telescope; and on a platform above was the range-finder, an instrument of powerful magnification. Within a commendably brief time after Sam had sounded the alarm, somewhere between fifteen and twenty seconds, there were manned six pairs of binoculars, two spyglasses, two long-glasses, of course the ship's telescope, and the range-finder. The glasses were all on the target right away, but the range-finder took a little longer, that instrument being a large unwieldy affair which required considerable frantic cranking and adjusting by two men in order to focus on a target. Through a rather surprising sense of delicacy, considering that two quartermasters and the talker were left without, one pair of binoculars remained untouched: the ones clearly labeled 'Captain.' In future scrutinies, it was found necessary to press all glasses into service, exempting none.

Sam's discovery was basically simple, natural, reasonable. He had discovered that nurses lived in the long, yellow house. He had discovered two large windows in the middle of the second-story front, and that these windows had none but shade curtains, retracted. He had discovered (the telescope is a powerful glass and the room was well illumined by sunlight) that the windows belonged to the bathroom. It is, of course, redundant to say that he had also discovered a nurse in the shower stall in the far left-hand corner of the room. All of this would seem to be a model of logic, of sweet reasonableness: what could possibly be more logical than that there be a hospital at this base, that there be nurses attached to this hospital, that these nurses lived in a house, that this house have a bathroom, that this bathroom have windows, that these nurses bathe? Nothing, you would think. And yet to these signalmen and quartermasters (who had last seen a white woman, probably fat, certainly fully clothed, perhaps fourteen months ago) this vision was literally that, a vision, and a miracle, and not a very small miracle, either. Like Sam, they were stricken with reverence in its presence, and like Sam, their remarks were reverent; those who could speak at all. 'Holy Christ!' a few of them managed to breathe, and 'Son-of-a-bitch!' That was all. Those are the only legitimate things a man can say when suddenly confronted with the imponderable.

The word spread fast, although how it is difficult to say: certainly no one left the bridge. The four-to-eight signal watch, Niesen and Canappa, never known to relieve before the stroke of the hour, appeared at three-thirty and met an equally incredible thing; a watch that refused to be relieved. 'Get the hell out of here,' Sam told the newcomers. 'We're staying up here till chow.' There was some bitterness and much indignant insistence by the oncoming pair of their *right* to relieve the watch, but the old watch, firmly entrenched at the glasses, stayed by them until chow was piped. There was a splendid run of bathers. The shore station blinked for half an hour trying to rouse this ship, a bare two hundred yards away; and, finally succeeding, sent out a nasty message about keeping a more alert signal watch. Accordingly, the glass of the striker Mannion was taken away from him and he was detailed to watch for signals. It seemed that Sam had just gone below for supper when he was back again, demanding and getting his telescope. He and the rest of the watch stayed on until after sunset, when lights went on in the bathroom and the curtains were pulled chastely down for the night; all the way down, leaving not the merest crack.

That first day was chaotic, comparable perhaps to the establishing of a beachhead. It was ill-organized; there was duplication and wasted effort. The next day went much better. A system and a pattern appeared. The curtain was raised at 0745 and was witnessed by Sam, Schlemmer, Canappa, Mannion, Morris, Niesen, three quartermasters, and the officer-of-the-deck. For perhaps forty-five minutes there was a dazzling crowd of early-morning bathers; almost a surfeit of them, sometimes three or four at a time. Then there was a long slack period (no one in the room) that extended to ten o'clock. Sam organized for the slack period. It is fatiguing to stand squinting through an eyepiece for long periods, so Sam arranged that one man, by turns, keep the lookout during the off-hours and give the word when action developed. But he refused to let Mannion take a turn. 'That son-of-a-bitch watched one strip down yesterday and didn't open his mouth,' he accused.

It was possible by this time to establish the routine of the house. After the big early-morning rush there was only an occasional and accidental visitor until around ten, when the night watch would begin to get up. From ten to eleven was fairly good, and eleven until noon was very good. From lunch until two was quiet, but from two until two-forty-five there was the same rich procession as in the morning. After four, things dropped off sharply and weren't really much good again for the rest of the day. It was shrewdly observed and duly noted that watches at the hospital evidently changed at eight in the morning and three in the afternoon. All glasses were manned during those periods; pathetic little two-power opera glasses made their appearance then, and the windshield and splinter-shields of the flying bridge presented a solid wall of variously magnified eyeballs.

By this time, also, the watch — as it came to be known — assumed a routine of its own. The assignment and ownership of glasses came to be understood. Three pairs of binoculars belonged down below for the officer-of-the-deck and two quartermasters. The other four pairs of binoculars, the spy-glasses and the long-glasses, belonged to the signalmen; to use themselves or lend to radiomen, storekeepers, and cooks in return for future favors. The range-finder came to be recognized as officer property and was almost continually manned by a rotating team of two officers; Lieutenant Carney and Ensign Moulton being the most constant. The big telescope, of course, was a prize. It magnified thirty-two times. There was a box of Lux soap sitting on a shelf on the far wall of the bathroom, and with the telescope Sam could make out with ease the big letters 'LUX' and below them, in smaller letters, the word 'Thrifty.' He could even almost make out the much smaller words in the lower left-hand corner of the box. The long-glass could barely make out the word 'Thrifty' and couldn't begin to make out the words in the corner. The spy-glasses and the binoculars couldn't even make out the word 'Thrifty.'

From the first, Sam's right to the telescope had been strangely unchallenged, perhaps in intuitive recognition of his zeal. Turncliffe, the first-class signalman, gave him a brief argument once — more of a token argument, really, than anything else — and then retired to the long-glass. For quite a while Sam was indisputably on the telescope; then one morning Lieutenant (jg) Billings chanced on the bridge. Lieutenant Billings was the communication officer and Sam's boss, and he relieved Sam briefly on the telescope. That was all right the first time; Sam was good-natured in yielding; he liked Mr. Billings. But then Mr. Billings began to chance on the bridge frequently and regularly, and every time he would relieve Sam. Not only that, he had an uncanny talent for arriving at the most propitious moment. Sam got pretty sore over the whole business. As he complained to his friend Schlemmer: 'Sure, he's an officer. All right. If we was in a chow line together, sure, he could go in ahead of me. All right. But I sure can't see where that gives him the right to take a man's glass away from him!' To Sam, a man's glass was an inviolable thing.

By the third day personalities began to emerge from the amorphous group that flitted past the bathroom windows. Despite the fact that the light was usually bad up around the face, thus eliminating facial identifications as a method, the boys were able to distinguish one nurse from another with considerable accuracy. There appeared to be nine consistent users of this particular bathroom. Canappa insisted there were only eight, but then he denied the validity of the two-blonde theory. The two-blonde theory was Sam's and it was supported by the consensus. Canappa pointed out that the two had never been seen together; but this was rather a foolish argument, as both had been examined separately from the same angle, which happened to be a telling one. Canappa, who had not seen both from this angle, stuck to his discredited opinion. Undeniably, there were grounds for confusion. Both girls were young, both were pretty (although, as mentioned before, facial characteristics were inexact), and both wore red-and-white striped bathrobes — or maybe even the same bathrobe. That is no doubt what threw Canappa off. Because, actually, there was conclusive evidence of their separate identity; evidence of the most distinctive sort which one of the girls carried.

As Mannion put it, looking up from his glass: 'What the hell is that she's got?'

Sam *didn't* look up from his glass. 'You dumb bastard, that's a birthmark.'

Mannion was convinced, but he was irritated by Sam's tone. 'Birthmark!' he said scornfully. 'Who the hell ever heard of a birthmark down there? That's paint; she's gotten into some paint. Or else it's a burn. That's what it is — it's a burn!'

Sam's rebuttal was simple and unanswerable: 'Who the hell ever heard of a burn down there?' It routed Mannion satisfactorily, and after a moment Sam disclosed: 'Why, Christ, I had an uncle once who had a birthmark . . . ' He went on to tell where his uncle's birthmark was situated. He described it in some detail.

The two blondes were the real stars: as the result of comparison the other girls came to be regarded as rather run-of-the-mill and were observed with condescension and even some small degree of indifference. There was one, rather old and quite fat, who absolutely disgusted Schlemmer. Whenever she put in an appearance, he would leave his glass and indignantly exhort the rest of the watch to do the same. 'Don't look at her,' he would say. 'She's nausorating!' He got quite angry when he was ignored.

With the emergence of personalities came the recognition of personal habits. The tall skinny brunette al-

ways let the shower water run for several minutes before a bath. The stubby little brunette with the yellow
bathrobe always used the bathtub; would sit in the tub
and drink what looked like coffee, but might have been
tea. The girl with high, piled-up hair would fuss for
an hour extracting hairpins, and then take a shampoo
in the washbasin by the window without removing her
robe. 'That's a stupid goddamn way to take a shampoo,' Sam commented.

But by far the most notable idiosyncrasy belonged
to the blonde with the birthmark. It was one which en-
deared her to all the watchers and drove Morris to rap-
turously announce: 'I'm going to marry that gal!' Like
everything about the place it was plausible, normal, and
really not at all remarkable. It occurred before every
bath and consisted simply of shedding the red-and-
white striped bathrobe and standing for several minutes (discreetly withdrawn from the window), looking
out over the bay. Undoubtedly, this was a girl who
loved beauty, and certainly the view was a fine one.
The bay in the afternoon was shiny blue plate glass,
really perfect except where the wake of a lazily paddled
native canoe flawed the illusion. The tall coconut palms
along the beach were as poetically motionless as sculp-
ture. A little way out from the bay was the thin white
line of the surf at the reef, and far, far out was the
scary, almost indistinguishable line of the horizon.
Perhaps the girl's thoughts, as she stood admiring all
that beatitude, ran something like this: 'What peace!
There is no effort anywhere. See the canoe drifting

lazily across the bay. Observe the trees with not a
leaf stirring, and the ship riding peacefully at anchor,
her men justly resting after the arduous days at sea.
What utter tranquillity!' From there she could not hear
the cranking of the range-finder.

There was one ghastly afternoon when not a soul,
not a single soul, came in for a bath. The watchers
were bewildered and resentful; and, finally, disgusted.
Sam probably spoke for all when he said: 'Christ, and
they call themselves nurses! They're nothing but a
goddamn bunch of filthy pigs. A nurse would at least
take a bath once in a while. Jesus, I pity those poor
sick bastards over there who have to let those filthy pigs
handle them!'

But that only happened once, and by and large it
could not fairly be said that the nurses were disappointing. In fact, Sam himself was once moved to observe: 'This is too good to last.' It was one of the most
prophetic things Sam ever said.

Lieutenant (jg) Langston, the gunnery officer, had
been having a good bit of trouble with his eyes. He
wasn't at all satisfied with his glasses. One day he had
a splitting headache and the next morning he went over
to the base hospital to have his eyes refracted. They
were very nice over there. The Doctor was very nice,
and there was a pleasant-faced nurse who helped, and
she also was very nice. It took only about an hour and
a half to find just the right lenses, and while he was
waiting for his pupils to contract, Langston began talk-

ing with the nurse. In a very short time it came out that she was from a town not twenty miles from Youngstown, Ohio, where he lived. Langston felt that a certain bond was established, and on the strength of it he invited the nurse, whose name was Miss William-son, to dinner on the ship that night. It is well known that shipboard food is several cuts above shore-based food, and this consideration was perhaps a factor in Miss Williamson's ready acceptance. She did add one clause, though: she asked if she could bring a friend, 'a terribly cute girl.' Langston, a personable if rather courtly young man, of course said yes, and mentioned that he would assign her to a friend of his, an Ensign Pulver, whom he described as a 'very handsome young man.' Everything was most friendly.

When the girls came aboard that night, escorted by the two officers, the entire crew was massed along the rail and on the bridges. As the white-stockinged legs tripped up the gangway, one great, composite, heart-felt whistle rose to the heavens and hung there. Ensign Pulver's girl, Miss Girard, had turned out to be a knockout. At dinner in the wardroom he could scarcely keep his eyes off her, and no more could the other officers, who feigned eating and made self-conscious conversation. Miss Girard had lovely soft blond hair which she wore in bangs, wide blue innocent eyes, and the pertest nose there ever was. The total effect was that of radiant innocence; innocence triumphant. Only Ensign Pulver noted that when she smiled her eyes screwed up shrewdly and her mouth curved knowingly;

but then only Ensign Pulver would. For Langston, it was enough to have what he felt to be the envious admiration of his messmates; but there began to grow in the mind of Ensign Pulver, himself a young man of deceptively guileless appearance, visions of a greater reward. Once in a while he would catch and hold Miss Girard's glance, and when he did he thought he detected interest there.

After dinner, when the party repaired to his room for further polite conversation, he felt more and more sure of it. There were only two chairs in the room and so he and Miss Girard sat together on the edge of the bottom bunk. That gave a certain intimacy, he thought; a certain tie of shared experience. He was moved to break out the quart of Old Overholt, four-fifths full, which he had kept hidden for two months in the little recess under the drawer of his bunk. With Coca-Cola which Langston provided it made a nice drink. Ensign Pulver was then emboldened to tell what he privately called his 'test story,' the decisively off-color tale of 'ze black chapeau.' Miss Girard's response was excellent; she laughed delightedly. Then, craftily aware of the impressiveness of the unfamiliar, he proposed a tour of the ship, and both girls enthusiastically approved. The plan now began to shape itself in Pulver's mind: after the tour, a few more drinks; then a little dancing in the wardroom; then a few more drinks; then get Langston to take the other one off somewhere. As they started out, Miss Girard gave him her small hand.

First they toured the main deck, the offices and

the galley and sick bay. Then they dropped down into the cavernous engine room, and Pulver, who was an engineering officer, talked casually of the massive turbines and terrifying boilers. The girls were very much impressed. From the engine room they went up to the bridge, through the wheelhouse, through the charthouse, through the radio room, and on up to the flying bridge. That was a thoughtless thing for the two officers to do, but fortunately an alert quartermaster had preceded them. The inspection party found the signalmen clustered in an innocent group under the canvas awning, and the telescope trained at an angle of ninety degrees from the yellow house. The signalmen presented a curious sight. They were absolutely speechless; they seemed welded to the deck with awe. The two nurses giggled a little, no doubt over the prospect of these men so obviously dumbfounded at seeing a woman that they could only gape. Ensign Pulver later claimed that he felt something ominous in that group, but whether or not he actually did is unimportant.

Langston led the party to the forward splintershield, where it could look down the sheer drop to the main deck, and the even more scary distance to the very bottom of number three hatch. The girls were *really* impressed with that. When they started to walk around behind the funnel, Ensign Pulver noticed that Sam Insigna was trailing them. He was a little annoyed, but, being a young man of poise, he made a sort of introduction. 'This is Sam,' he said, 'one of the signalmen.'

Miss Girard smiled at Sam. 'How do you do, Sam,'

she said graciously. Sam was evidently too shy and flustered to speak; he just stood there and grinned foolishly. When they had gone on, Miss Girard squeezed her escort's hand and whispered, 'He's darling.' Pulver nodded dubiously. They took a turn around the funnel, came forward again, and went over to the port wing to look at the twenty-millimeters. By this time the signalmen had gotten their tongues back and were having a bitter and quite vocal argument under the awning. It was obvious that they were trying to keep their voices guarded, but, as often happens, the restraint only intensified them. Sam's voice in particular carried well. 'Goddamit,' the party heard him say, 'I'll bet you one hundred bucks!' Lieutenant (jg) Langston nodded his head in the direction of the signalmen, smiled superiorly, and said to the nurses: 'Seems to be an argument.' Then Sam's voice came to them again. That voice was several things: it was shrill, it was combative, it was angry; but most of all it was audible. There have been few more audible voices, before or since. It traveled out from under the awning in an unfaltering parabola, fell on the ears of the inspection party, and broke into words of simple eloquence.

'You stupid son-of-a-bitch, I tell you that's her! I got one hundred bucks that says that's the one with the birthmark on her ass! Now put up or shut up!'

Sam may have been right, at that. No one ever knew; no one on the ship ever saw that birthmark again. The curtains of the two middle upstairs windows were not raised next morning, and when the ship sailed three days later they were still down. It was three weeks before a sizable membership of the crew would speak to Sam except to curse him, and it was longer than that before Ensign Pulver would speak to him at all.

ALL OF THE OFFICERS, excepting the Doctor and Mr. Gonaud, the supply officer, had at one time or another submitted letters to the Bureau requesting a change of duty. This was their privilege, and presumably the Bureau gave just consideration to such letters. These officers, however, turned in their requests perfunctorily and without hope; for all of them were absolutely certain that there existed at the Bureau a yeoman, probably a Wave, whose sole duty it was to drop all such correspondence, unopened, into a roaring incinerator. As incontestable proof of this theory they cited that in fourteen months the only officer transferred had been an ensign named Soucek, who had been aboard only six months and who had never submitted a letter. Naturally there was some ill-will toward Soucek, who was considered underserving of such spectacular good fortune; but for the most part the officers accepted the stroke philosophically and even, their theory confirmed, with a certain satisfaction.

While the officers may or may not have been right in guessing the disposition of their requests, there can be no doubt at all that they correctly gauged the futility of them. As a matter of policy — a policy, clearly, of pure spite; since he had loudly and many times expressed his desire to be rid of his whole passel of officers — the Captain always forwarded these letters with the endorsement: 'Not recommending approval.' That way they were licked from the start.

The other officers were content to submit their one letter, make their one gesture, and let it go at that, but Lieutenant Roberts did not give up so easily. One month to the day after he had written his first request, he appeared in the yeoman's office and had the letter retyped verbatim and presented again to the Captain. The Captain muttered, then sputtered, then roared: but he had no choice other than to forward it; with, of course, the same negative endorsement. Every month after that — without fail, it was exactly a month — this procedure was repeated: Lieutenant Roberts would submit the same letter and the Captain with the same curses would apply the same endorsement. It might seem that this was a foolish and futile business and in the main Roberts would agree; but not entirely. As he explained to his friend Ensign Pulver, he felt it had a certain nuisance value. He reasoned that if anyone at the Bureau did indeed read these letters, sooner or later that person was going to get so very angry that he would be transferred to the naval equivalent of Siberia — which, by comparison with the *Reluctant*, he did not consider at all undesirable. And he knew for an agreeable fact that every time the yeoman appeared bearing his letter, the Captain's digestion was effectively ruined for at least one meal.

Roberts submitted these letters so regularly on the fourteenth of each month that once, when he forgot, Steuben, the yeoman, came around and in some alarm reminded him that his letter was due.

There was an incident one day with the Captain which served to demonstrate to Roberts that he was wedded to this ship irrevocably and for all time, that there was nothing in the world he could do to release himself, and that his only hope for separation lay in the direct intervention of God. Like most incidents between the officers and the Captain, it occurred while Roberts had the O.O.D. watch in port.

As with every other detail of life aboard the *Reluctant,* there was a ritual for these incidents. The Captain would sit all day in his cabin and through his portholes scan the foredeck. Whenever he saw there something that displeased him — a matter of ridiculous ease — he would vigorously so inform the officer-of-the-deck. Sometimes he would make these notices the matter of a personal visit to the bridge, and at others he would deliver them by telephone. Allowing for the small variety of occasion, these monologues were remarkably of a type; they were invariably profane, unfailingly shrill, and always they concluded with the threat of ten days in hack for the officer-of-the-deck.

Ten days in hack means for an officer ten days' confinement in his room, and in the Old Navy, the Regular Navy, it was considered a drastic punishment. An officer thus punished was considered to be publicly humiliated, and undoubtedly felt that way himself. This punishment was viewed in a somewhat different light by the Reserve officers of the *Reluctant.* To say that ten days in hack was considered a reward of almost unbearable loveliness is not to exaggerate. The Captain had carried out his threat with only one officer, Carney, and Carney had had a wonderful time in his room. He slept happily for most of the ten days, getting up only to eat, to work on his water colors, or to entertain the almost continuous stream of envious officers who visited him. If the Captain had been at all a perceptive man, he would have seen that with these officers his threat was not the proper one.

On this afternoon Roberts had had a very busy watch. The ship was simultaneously unloading cargo from three holds onto LCM's and LCT's, and he had not only the routine of the watch, but also the complex duties of cargo officer to occupy him. He had to see that the boats tied up at the right place, that they were loaded properly, and, since there was need for speed, that the whole operation kept moving. It is a complicated and highly trying business, moving cargo onto half a dozen landing craft at one time, and Roberts's patience would have been strained even without the series of petty interference from the Captain. Normally the Captain had just enough sense to leave Roberts alone — except for a little nagging in a routine way to keep up appearances — but today he clearly forgot himself. If he had called the bridge once this afternoon, he had called fifteen times, and every time Roberts had to drop what he was doing and listen to the Old Man's views on some such absurd detail as a man on deck without a cap, or cigarette butts on the flying bridge. Roberts had a fair store of patience, but the Captain was going through it fast.

The last time the Captain called Roberts was out on the wing telling three different boats where he wanted them. He refused to talk to the Captain. 'Tell him I'm busy!' he said to the quartermaster. The quartermaster did that and came back grinning. 'Flash Red!' he announced. In the usages of the ship this meant, not that an air attack was imminent, but rather a visit from the Captain. A second later the Captain stormed onto the wing. As always when in extreme anger, his face was beet-red.

He shouted at Roberts. 'What the hell do you mean, telling me you're busy? Who the hell do you think you are anyhow? By God, I'm running this here ship and when I tell you I want to talk to you, by God, you get on that phone in a goddamn quick hurry! Do you understand?'

Roberts had been standing in the outboard corner of the wing with a megaphone in his hand. He put the megaphone down very carefully and turned to the Captain. 'Captain,' he said easily, 'there's no use your coming up here and getting all excited. We're doing this job as well as we can, and if you just leave us alone and quit bothering, we'll get along all right.' And with that he picked up the megaphone and shouted instructions to an LCT.

Bergstrom, the quartermaster, and the messenger and the talker were all right there and they saw the whole thing. They told later how the Captain's eyes popped almost out of his head, how his mouth fell open, and how for a space of several seconds it worked soundlessly. Then he was shouting again, and shaking his fist at Roberts, and absolutely quivering with rage.

'Now you've gone too far! You've gone too far this time! By God, you can't talk to me like that and get away with it! By God, I'm the Captain of this ship, and no smart son-of-a-bitching college officer is going to talk like that! I don't have to put up with crap like that and I don't intend to! You can go in your room for ten days and see how you like that!'

Roberts had slung around his neck a pair of binoculars, which he had been using for spotting the numbers
of approaching boats. He faced the Captain now and
removed the glasses. 'Do you relieve me, Captain!' he
said coldly. 'Can I go down in my room now? I'd like
ten days in my room, you know!'

The Captain's mouth worked again, and then he said:
'Yeah, I know you would! You think you're pretty goddamn smart, don't you?'

'Are you relieving me, Captain?' Roberts persisted.
'Are you giving me ten days in hack? Can I start now,
Captain?' He extended the glasses to the Captain.

Captain Morton had deflated visibly now. A slightly
trapped look had come into his face. He didn't look at
Roberts and he didn't shout. He looked uneasily out
over the water. He ignored the proffered glasses. 'By
God,' he said defensively and quite inconsistently, 'I
don't ask a lot from you officers, but when I want a
thing done I want it done! Now, by God, you just do
your job and don't go trying to tell me how to run this
here ship and we'll get along all right. But, by God,
I'm not going to take a lot of crap from you officers!'

The Captain turned then and started to slouch away,
but Roberts was implacable.

'How about it, Captain?' he demanded. 'Am I going
in my room for ten days or not?'

The Captain's face filled with blood again, but still
he didn't turn around to Roberts. 'By God,' he muttered
fiercely, 'I'll let you know when I give you ten days
and, by God, you'll know it! Now you just get to work

and take care of your job up here!' And the Captain started walking away into the wheelhouse.

Roberts stayed right at his heels. 'Captain, if you don't like the way I'm handling my job, why don't you get me transferred? You could do it, you know, Captain!'

Captain Morton was now in complete rout. It was public rout, too, for suddenly there were half a dozen enlisted men in the wheelhouse. He didn't turn even now to make a stand. 'By God, you just take care of your job and don't go trying to run the ship,' he mumbled again, and he kept on walking toward the door.

Roberts was as relentless as a Fury. 'It would be easy, Captain,' he went on. 'All you have to do is write a letter and say you want to get rid of me. I'll even write the letter *for* you, Captain!' he offered.

But the Captain, trailing an unintelligible mutter, had ducked quickly through the door and down the ladder.

The incident was an instantaneous sensation on the ship. Everyone talked of it, and Roberts's name was on everyone's lips. He could not conceivably have been more of a hero. Everywhere he went, hands were thrust into his and he was effusively congratulated. To the crew of the *Reluctant*, it seemed a splendid victory.

But Roberts didn't see it that way. That night Ensign Pulver, sitting talking in his room, said to him: 'Boy, you really won a round today!'

And Roberts shook his head thoughtfully and answered: 'No, I didn't win. He won.'

'How the hell do you figure?' Pulver demanded.

Roberts turned up his palms. 'I'm still on the ship,' he pointed out. Then he said wearily: 'No, Pulver, he won. He wins them all. The Captain's bound to win, every time.'

T HIS HAPPENED on a very hot day. It was shortly after
noon, about one o'clock, and the sick, white-hot sun
was slamming down from almost directly overhead. But
for a few scattered puffy cirrus clouds the sky was clear,
and it was almost colorless. Even at its zenith the sun

had faded it to pallid blue, and lower down, all the way around the horizon, it was bleached to a dead, dirty white. The sea wasn't blue either, but a sudden uniform shine crawling in all directions to the flawed line of the horizon. There was no breeze; even the ten-knot motion of the ship didn't create any. The air was as stored, baled, stagnant as that of an attic room on a summer day. The deck and all of the metal surfaces of the ship were scalding to the feet and to the touch. Except directly beneath the gun tubs and close against the mast-tables and the house there was no shade.

The gun crew of the forward three-inch battery was miserable. Big Gerhart, the gun captain, and Wiley, the third-class gunner's mate, stood leaning on the pointer's seat. Red Stevens was standing with his elbows propped on the splintershield looking out to starboard. Reber, wearing the headset, was also propped against the splintershield facing aft. The fifth man, little Porky Payne, was stationed over on the port gun, ostensibly keeping a lookout in that direction. All of them were on their feet because they were right there under the Captain's eye all the time. For the same reason all of them kept their dungaree shirts on and all of their shirts were sweated soaking wet. That was the hell of being up here where the Old Man could see you. The five-inch crew back aft could sit down in the shade, if there was any, and take off their shirts; but not up here. Big Gerhart wiped the sweat from his face and flicked it away. 'Christ!' he said. His hair was cropped short and his eyes were small and pig-like in a round,

small-featured face. He walked to the forward edge of
the gun tub and looked down. Below him a couple of
first division men were lying in the shade with their
heads cradled on life-jackets. Lady, the terrier-bull-
dog-spaniel, was flattened on her stomach in a little
puddle of shade on the hatch-cover. Her tongue was
out and flopping from the side of her mouth as she lay
head down, panting.

'Christ!' Gerhart said again, and then, 'To hell with
it!' He jerked open his shirt, stripped it off and flung it
over the pointer's seat. His fat white back was greasy
with sweat. 'To hell with it,' he announced. 'I'll be goddamned if I'm going to keep a shirt on today!' Nobody
said anything.

He stood for a moment leaning over the splintershield. 'Hey, Whitley,' he called to one of the men
lying below him, 'pass the dog up here.' Grumbling, the
man picked up the limp little dog and passed her up
the ladder to Gerhart. Wiley watched disapprovingly.
'Why the hell don't you leave her alone?' he said.
Gerhart said, 'Shut up,' and knelt beside the dog.

The dog looked up at him with pleading, infinitely
weary eyes. He started talking to her. 'What do you
say, Lady? How're you getting along?' He prodded
her in the ribs. He rolled her over on her back and
started slapping her stomach sharply. His lips
clenched tightly as he did this. 'What's the matter,
Lady?' he said. 'What ya lying around like that for?
Didn't you get the word? "Turn to," they said, "turn
to." ' He pulled the dog to her feet, grasped her two

front paws and started waltzing her about. 'That's the stuff, Lady,' he said. 'You got to step lively in this here outfit. Got to get off your ass.'

Wiley said again: 'For Christ's sake, leave the dog alone! Can't you see she's half dead!'

Gerhart looked up coldly. 'Why don't you mind your own business?' He turned again to the dog. 'Eh, Lady,' he said. He took her then by the hind legs and wheeled her from side to side. She was panting in quick, fierce gasps and saliva ran from her mouth. 'Yessir, Lady,' said Gerhart, 'you're getting out of shape. Sit around on your ass too much. Got to get off your ass in this outfit.' Finally he allowed her to lie down on the deck. He took her then by the ears and jerked her head from side to side, first by yanking one ear, then the other. The little dog whined in pain. Gerhart gave one last tug. 'Okay, Lady,' he said, 'you're a cry-baby. Go back and lie on your ass.' He stood up and left the dog lying on the hot deck. Wiley picked her up and stepped down the ladder and put her in the shade of the gun tub. 'Jesus Christ!' he said disgustedly.

The gun crew stood in heavy, sodden silence. They hardly moved, seemed hardly to breathe. Once Gerhart slapped at his stomach as a drop of sweat rolled down. There was no let-up to the lidless sun, and the heated air settled with almost palpable weight. The gun crew slumped beneath it. Gerhart and Wiley leaned hard against the pointer's seat. Red Stevens stood staring bewitched at the water. Reber, the talker, hitched at his binding pants around the crotch.

Somewhere back aft a chipping hammer was being worked; otherwise there was no sound but the hiss that the bow made as it slid through the viscous water. The surface writhed with heat waves, and it was possible to see upon it many things that weren't there at all.

'What time is it?' Gerhart said suddenly. 'Must be after two.'

'It is like hell,' said Wiley. 'It's ten after one.'

'Jesus!' said Gerhart. 'Is that all it is? Let me see.' He grabbed Wiley's arm and looked at the watch. 'Jesus!' he said. 'I thought sure it was two anyhow.' He shook his head and turned and walked around the gun.

Reber put his hand to the mouthpiece of his headset. 'Three-inch, aye aye,' he said into it. Then he listened for a moment. The others watched him incuriously. 'Aye aye,' he said again. He took his hand away from the mouthpiece and announced: 'The Captain says to tell Gerhart he's on report and to get his shirt on in a damn quick hurry.'

Gerhart's red face got very red all the way down to the white line of his neck. He grabbed his shirt and almost ripped it off the seat. 'On report!' he snarled as he struggled into the shirt. 'That miserable bastard! That dirty miserable son-of-a-bitch! I wonder if he thinks he's getting a cherry!' He turned around, facing aft, and looked fiercely up at the wings of the bridge and the portholes of the wheelhouse.

'Better watch out,' said Wiley. 'He's probably got the glasses trained right on you reading everything you say.'

Gerhart's lip curled back in a sneer. 'I don't give a goddamn what he's doing! If he wants to come down here I'll tell the son-of-a-bitch to his face! Any miserable bastard that'd make a man wear a shirt out here today ought to get the hell kicked out of him. Jesus!' He spat on the deck. He picked up a block of wood under the ready box and flung it over the side. 'Jesus!' he said. He started pacing up and down the catwalk between the two guns.

'What a miserable screwing outfit!' he muttered. 'What a miserable screwing life!'

All this time Red Stevens had been standing at the starboard edge of the gun tub looking down into the water. Gerhart walked over to him now and stopped, hands on his hips. 'What the hell are you looking at, bright eyes?' he demanded.

Red Stevens was a boy of twenty or twenty-one with orange hair and freckles, and although he was very shy he was well-liked. He was the best-natured kid on the ship, and so he always took a lot of ribbing. But he always took it. He was so shy that no matter what was said to him he would grin and blush. He grinned now at Big Gerhart. 'I was watching the flying fish,' he said softly.

'Oh, you was watching the flying fish!' Gerhart mimicked. 'Well, ain't that nice! How long you been out here, anyhow?'

Red blushed. 'Eleven months,' he said.

'Eleven months,' said Gerhart. 'Eleven months and you're already watching the flying fish! Boy, when you finish up your five years out here, you'll *really* be Asiatic! You'll really be seeing flying fish then!'

Wiley walked over and joined in. 'Red can't stay out here no five years,' he said. 'He's got to get back to his wife.'

Gerhart snorted. 'Get back to his wife, hell! They got it ten years out here now for married men.' He stopped and looked at Red. 'Are you married, Red?' he asked with sudden interest.

Red started to blush, and Wiley answered for him. 'Sure he's married. The cutest little doll you ever saw. Show him her picture, Red,' he said.

'Yeah?' said Gerhart. 'You got a picture of her, Red?'

'Sure,' said Wiley. 'Show him the picture, Red.'

Very embarrassed, Red got out his wallet and passed it to Gerhart. Gerhart stood and studied the pictures. He let out a long whistle. He smacked his lips. 'Mm-mmmh,' he said, 'that's *all* right. That's all right, boy. Where'd you ever get a gal like that?' He looked again at the wallet before passing it back. 'Man, that bathing suit gets me!'

His voice became easy and conversational. 'How long you been married, Red?'

Red smiled, 'About fourteen months.'

'Yeah?' said Gerhart. 'You was married about two months before you come out here?'

Red nodded.

'Your wife, how old would she be? About twenty?'

'She's twenty now. She was nineteen then.'

'What's her name by the way?'

'Margie.'

'Margie,' said Gerhart. 'That's a nice name. Where did you and Margie go on your honeymoon?'

Wiley said: 'All right, Gerhart, don't go getting started on Red's wife.' His voice, though, didn't really protest and he continued to stand by listening with a half-smile.

Gerhart ignored him. 'Where did you and Margie go for the first night you was married?' he went on.

Red blushed. 'San José,' he said. 'That's where we were married.'

'San José, huh? Well, that's a nice town. Did you stay at a hotel there?'

Red nodded and looked down at the water.

Gerhart's voice got confidential. 'Tell me something, Red,' he said. 'I ain't married myself and I've always wondered. How was it that first night? Huh?'

Red blushed deeply. 'How do you mean?' he said.

Gerhart prodded him in the ribs and winked. 'You know how I mean. How was it?'

Red started to say something and then stopped. 'Okay,' he said finally.

'Okay?' said Gerhart. 'Well, that's fine. Tell me,' he went on, 'how many times did you do it that first night, Red?'

Red didn't look up. 'I don't know.'

'Oh, sure you know. How many times was it?'

'I don't remember.'

'You don't remember? Jesus, a pretty girl like that, I'd sure remember it!'

Red didn't say anything. He was absorbedly peeling paint off the outside of the splintershield.

'Say, tell me something,' Gerhart said smoothly. 'Was your wife a virgin when you was married? I mean I'm just an old country boy and I want to find out about these things, so when I get married.'

Red looked up quickly at Big Gerhart. Then he looked puzzledly over to Wiley. He started a smile and then stopped. 'Naturally,' he said.

'Hey,' said Wiley, 'for Christ's sake knock it off. That's none of your damn business.'

'Shut up,' said Gerhart. He turned again to Red. 'So Margie was a virgin. Well, I'm glad to hear that. So many girls ain't these days, you know.' He rubbed his chin thoughtfully. 'How did Margie like it that first night?'

Red's blush by now had turned to a deep, solid flush. 'I don't know,' he said shortly.

'Oh, sure you do,' Gerhart coaxed. 'What did she do — did she just lie there and whimper?'

'I don't know,' Red said. He kept looking out at the horizon.

Gerhart took on an offended tone. 'Aw, Red,' he said, 'you ain't any help at all. How am I going to know what to do when I get married if you ain't going to tell me things? You, an old married man like you are.'

Red gave a twisted smile and shook his head.

Gerhart went on: 'This is something they tell me is important, Red: were you able to keep her satisfied? A young, pretty girl like that?'

Red looked up quickly. He gave a strained little laugh. 'That's none of your business,' he said unconvincingly.

'Oh, sure it is,' Gerhart soothed. 'I want to find out about these things. I'm just an old country boy. Come on, Red, cut me in on the dope.'

'Don't tell him nothing, Red,' said Wiley. 'He's getting too damn nosey.' But Wiley kept smiling.

Gerhart didn't pay any attention. He continued softly: 'You know what they tell me, Red? They tell me that once a woman has had a little, she just can't get enough after that. Is that true?'

Red didn't answer.

'Yessir,' said Gerhart. 'That's what they tell me. How long did you say you'd been out here? Eleven months?'

Red said nothing.

'Okay, say eleven months. Now your wife Margie, she looks like a nice, normal healthy girl. She got the same desires the rest of us got — hell, Red, there's nothing wrong with that. You know, Red,' he finished, 'eleven months is a long time.'

Gerhart wiped the sweat from his face with a large flat hand and then he said: 'Tell me honestly, Red — now tell me the truth. Do you really expect Margie to be faithful to you all the time you're out here? Things being like they are? Now do you honestly?'

Red had a startled look. He looked quickly at Gerhart and then over at Wiley, standing beside him, and then his eyes darted around the gun tub. He licked his lips quickly and he didn't say anything.

Gerhart was smiling kindly and saying: 'Now I don't mean no disrespect to Margie. I think Margie's a fine girl. Yessir, a fine girl.' His voice became paternally gentle. 'But you know how things are, Red. Here you are, way out here. You've been away eleven months. You'll be out here a hell of a lot longer. Margie, she's a normal healthy girl. She's got those desires same as all of us. Hell, Red, you can't blame her if she has a little fun once in a while. A pretty girl like that. No sir, you got to figure on it. Why, I bet you right now, Red, while we're standing here, Margie might be dropping her pants and crawling into bed . . .'

That was when Red hit him. Wiley saw it coming, but he moved too late to stop it. There was a spanner wrench lying on top of the ready box just aft of the gun. It was two steps away from Red. Before Wiley could even raise his hand, Red had taken those two steps, grabbed the wrench, and hit Gerhart with it on the side of the head as hard as he could. He was drawing his arm back to hit Gerhart again when Wiley finally was able to move, and he grabbed Red's arm and stopped him. Gerhart curled up and dropped to the deck and the blood was running from his head. And all the time Red hadn't said one word or made a sound. He was actually smiling when Wiley took the wrench away from him.

It took thirteen stitches to close up the side of Gerhart's head and he was in sick-bay for a week. Red got a summary court-martial, but the officers on the court were sympathetic and he was only fined twenty-five dollars. Big Gerhart, as soon as he was up and around, started threatening that he would take Red apart, but the crew was all on Red's side, and it was made amply clear to Gerhart that he would do nothing of the sort. In fact, the only result of the incident, except for the stitches and the fine, was that Red was shifted to the five-inch gun crew. And the only result of that was that on a hot day the watches went slower than ever for Big Gerhart up on the three-inch.

The crew was certainly ripe for a good liberty when the *Reluctant* got orders to sail to Elysium in the Limbo Islands. The ship was three years out of the States and of her original crew there were only four members left. These were Johnson, the chief master-at-arms, and Yarby, the chief yeoman, and Olson and Dowdy. These four could and often did talk of liberties spent together in Boston and New York and Philly and Trinidad and Panama; and the crew would listen, excluded and jealous, to this reminiscence, and they would feel the unity and completeness of the four, and then they would go away sad — certain that this was something they would never have. In three years, their total liberty had consisted of three afternoon recreation parties on one of the inevitable islands, at which a couple of bottles of beer per man were doled out, and where a few of the more frustrated played a listless game of softball. That wasn't liberty — it was mockery of the word. The crew lived together and worked together and were bored together; they needed to play together, to remember playing together, and to be able to talk about having played together. Where was the tie of solidarity working in the smothering bottom of the hold? What was the bond of union standing the heated watches? They needed to raise hell together. So the news that they were going, not to Apathy again, nor to Tedium, nor to Ennui, but rather to Elysium, shook the crew like an explosion.

The word spread as infallibly as a pestilence, and a great deal faster. Not more than fifteen minutes after Lieutenant (jg) Billings, the communicator, got the inspired message, everyone on the ship knew about it. 'Hey, did you get the word?' men shouted at one another. 'This bucket's going to Elysium!' And with The Word were passed the few available facts on the place:

that it was down in a nice climate, well away from the
Equator, and that it was a lovely, civilized town of
thirty thousand population, a British colonial town, and
in peacetime quite a celebrated tourist stop on the
steamer track from Australia to the States. As soon as
the bald Word and these preliminary facts were
thoroughly disseminated, the crew set to work to get
additional information. They questioned all, and finally
found one man who had been to Elysium in peacetime.
That was Dowdy. Dowdy immediately became the
target of a barrage of excited questions.

With the first-comers he tried to answer civilly and
factually. Yes, it used to be a nice place; although he
didn't know what it was like now with the Army there.
The only women you could get were the natives, and
most of them were dark and pretty rough. Some of
them, though, were real beauties. Yes, there used to be
plenty of whore-houses, but the Army probably closed
them up. Maybe a few running on the sly. Liquor? —
the liquor's lousy. In peacetime all they had was island
gin and whiskey made from sugar-cane, and things
would be even worse now. 'That whiskey they make,'
said Dowdy, 'is really panther-piss. Two drinks of that
will knock you on your ass like nothing you ever saw!'

Dowdy was patient at first, but he was never patient
for very long, and soon he tired of being a Baedeker.
The questioners persisted all day, and they interfered
with his work. His answers grew short, and then sarcastic, and finally inaccurate. The girls, he told them,
were all very beautiful and promiscuous. The prices

ranged from one to six shillings. All you had to do was step into a souvenir shop and announce that you wanted to see the turquoise necklaces. Dowdy did the boys no service with this information. Their natural, unencouraged expectations of Elysium were unreasonable enough without any prodding.

The atmosphere of the ship was normally not what you would call electric. It fell a little short of that. But now, on the nine-day run to Elysium, there was an unmistakable galvanism in the air. It manifested itself in many distinctive ways. You would have a clue to it in the suits of whites, most of them brand-new and never-worn, that were broken out of lockers and seabags. You could have detected it in the sudden passion for shining shoes, ordinarily an affectation as neglected as manicuring. Louie Wilkes, the barber, could have told you something was up from the fact that he now worked twelve hours a day cutting hair. Normally he got customers only during working hours on busy deck days. The ship's canteen could have furnished the incontrovertible evidence: the sale during the first two days of the eighteen jars of Mum which it had carried in stock for three years. Another conclusive indication was the sudden boom in prophylactics, also a very neglected item on the shelves of the canteen. (There was much bitterness about these prophylactics; they were so old, had been carried in stock for so long, that when the crew tested them by filling with water about ninety per cent turned out to be defective.)

In these rather direct ways the crew was getting

ready for a liberty. One of the mess cooks hung a calendar in the messhall and every night with much ceremony he would X out a day. There was a red circle drawn around the ninth, the date of arrival. Stefanowski got fifty men to chip in five dollars apiece to an anchor pool, the first time in two years that any interest had been demonstrated in the time of the ship's arrival. At night after the tables had been cleared away, the crew would gather in the messhall, in little groups and in large groups, and talk and plot and plan. Everything was planned to the nicest detail. Cliques were formed, costs were calculated, obstacles were considered, individual projects were announced. No military campaign was ever more elaborately prepared for.

There was one curious and, as it turned out, ironic thing about the crew's plans for Elysium: the way, by their very nature — violent, carnal, orgiastic — that they precluded David Bookser from participation. This was not intentional on the part of the crew — they liked Bookser to a man — but since there was such unanimous agreement on a program that included no spiritual values, they just automatically counted him out. He represented the spirit on the *Reluctant* and it was rather lonely and valiant of him to do this. David Bookser, a seaman in the first division, was a beautiful boy. He *looked* spiritual: he was a pure Adonis: his features were fine and flawless, his skin almost transparently white, and his blond hair grew carelessly about his head in graceful ringlets. He did not look effeminate, though, and the crew did not regard him that way.

They were a little stunned by his beauty, even the dullest clod of them, and they made a sort of pet of Bookser. He was a quiet, earnest boy, and a hard worker, and he was going to enter the ministry when he got out of the Navy. The one time the crew held a 'Happy Hour,' devoted almost entirely to skits of the broadest and most animalistic sort, Bookser stole the show with his poised, true singing of 'Adeste Fideles.'

Because the crew liked Bookser, they rode him a great deal; but he was a match for them. All the way to Elysium, because the Elysium erected in the mind of the crew seemed such a classic antithesis of Bookser, he came in for a lot of attention. It tickled the crew members, the idea of Bookser loose in this blazing Sodom they were going to.

'Hey, Booksie,' they would say, 'how about us making a liberty in Elysium? Dowdy says he knows just the girl for you.'

Or, more bluntly:

'Hey, Booksie, what do you say we go over and get laid? You and me, huh? How about it?'

Or, subtly:

'Hey, Booksie, how about selling me your liberty? You ain't going to be using it, are you?'

And Bookser would take all this and smile and say in his soft voice, not at all flustered: 'No, thanks. I think I'll just go over and walk around.' That was the way it went, all the way to Elysium.

The *Reluctant* sailed through cool blue days and shining blue water, and came at last to the Limbo

Islands of the Pacific. It reached them six hours ahead of schedule, and possibly it was speeded along by the intense well-wishing of the crew. At daylight there they were, the wonderful Limbos, a faint, water-color line hovering low along the horizon. The entire crew turned out and stood along the rail and watched this line emerge from insubstantial tracery into clear, solid mass, beautiful with trees and tall brown hills and green fields neatly criss-crossed in the valleys. They were lovely islands, like nothing the crew had ever seen in the Pacific. The ship, following the channel, slipped in close ashore, and now with the naked eye the men could make out houses perched on the slopes, and people moving about, and even the sex of the people. Before they thought, many exclaimed, 'Holy Christ, there's a woman, look!' And then they reflected, and remembered that a woman was now a commonplace — that these islands thronged with lovely women waiting for them — and they shut up, abashed. They stood quiet and watched, soaking up strange impressions, while the ship steamed along the coast. It was two hours later that the *Reluctant* rounded the tip of the island, swung wide in the stream, and there, then, scattered and bright in the bowl of the dark hills, was Elysium. The crew gasped.

And then they yelled. Elysium had very much taken their fancy. It ran up from the bay to the rim of the hills, red and green slate roofs and fine stucco houses pastel-shaded, and straight, narrow streets shady under tall trees, and it all had the warm, gay look of a water

color. There were handsome public buildings and even
two buildings of six or seven stories. There were cars
and people moving about. The crew pounded each
other on the back and yelled. They yelled, 'Elysium,
here I come!' and they yelled, 'Hey, Dowdy, where's
the whore-houses?' and they yelled, 'When does liberty
start?' The excitement was so extreme that when the
ship finally tied up to a dock shortly after noon, it
wasn't even commented upon that Stefanowski had
won his own anchor pool — two hundred and fifty
dollars.

Then began a maddening period of preparation and
of waiting. On the theory that it had at least a one-in-
three chance of making the liberty list, almost the
entire crew gathered in the compartment and stripped
down to scivvies, ready for a lightning change into
whites. Plans made eight days ago were affirmed and
reaffirmed. Money was borrowed. Dowdy was questioned exhaustively on the exact location of the whore-
houses. David Bookser was seriously approached by
five different people wanting to buy his liberty. 'When
the hell does liberty start?' was repeated everywhere
like an incantation.

There was one final twist of torture. It was all that
was needed: it had the effect of exploding the head of
steam. While the crew huddled in the compartment,
the word reached them that the Captain wasn't going
to grant any liberty. 'Screw them!' the Captain was
quoted as telling the exec. 'They try to screw me, now
I'll screw them!' The crew sat like dead men: they had

never even considered anything like this. That there might be poor liberty, yes; that it might be three- or even four-section liberty, yes; but that there not *be* liberty — no! But while they sat stunned, before they could even curse the Captain, there came a miraculous, inexplicable change in official plans, and the P.A. speaker squawked exultantly: 'Li-ber-ty . . . will commence . . . immediately . . . for the starboard section!' It was all right then; it was wonderfully all right! Two-section liberty! — even the port section took consolation in that. And the starboard section dived for its whites.

Lieutenant (jg) Ed Pauley, the officer-of-the-deck, had a hectic time at the gangway. At one time he had to inspect the liberty cards and check out seventy-three men of a seventy-four-man liberty list. They swarmed around the gangway and pushed and shoved and in general behaved exactly like men leaving a sinking ship by the only escape hatch. He breathed a sigh of relief when they were finally gone. Fifteen minutes later the last man on the list, David Bookser, came up to the gangway. Pauley checked him out.

'Well, take it easy, Booksie,' he grinned.

'Yes, sir,' Bookser promised.

Pauley watched him amusedly as he walked down the dock, all alone. 'Poor kid,' Pauley thought, 'what the hell's he going to do over there?' He smiled a little at the idea.

Lieutenant Carney said he hoped the ship never had another liberty if it meant watches like the one he had that night. Carney had the eight-to-twelve, and he caught it all. It was the first time he had really been busy since he came aboard. The Doctor, too, had more business in that four-hour span than in the total sick calls of the last year.

Lieutenant (jg) Langston, with the four-to-eight, had a quiet watch. There was only one minor incident, although a prophetic one. Ringgold of the third division staggered up the dock leading a goat by the halter and tried to bring the goat aboard. Langston intervened, and Ringgold and the goat wandered amiably off. That was the only thing on Langston's watch.

Carney had been on watch only five minutes when a Navy pickup truck stopped on the dock and two shore patrolmen piled out. In the back end were five bodies in white uniforms. 'These are your boys,' the shore patrol called, 'come and get 'em.' The gangway P.O. and the messenger dragged the five aboard, one by one. They were out cold, and because they were filthy with vomit and dirt, Carney ordered them laid out on top of number three hatch. They were soon to have a lot of company.

Ten minutes later the truck returned. It carried three more bodies in back, and in the front seat was Ringgold. The charge against him was stealing a goat. The shore patrol submitted it on a yellow slip to Carney. The bodies joined the others on top of number three.

The truck was back again in fifteen minutes, this time with twelve bodies. A few minutes later, Costello, three other first division men, and two M.P.'s piled out of an Army jeep. Costello and the boys were very cheerful, even though considerably cut up about the face and hands. The charge was stealing a jeep and hitting and killing a cow. The M.P.'s said there would probably be civil charges brought about the cow. They gave Carney another yellow slip.

The arrival of the bodies became a commonplace and background event. The shore patrol truck delivered them all night long until twelve o'clock. The largest single load was fifteen. After the first few loads, Carney broke out a five-man working party and kept it standing by at the gangway to carry the bodies aboard.

There was more business for the Doctor at nine o'clock when Stuzyuiski, a third division man, weaved up the dock accompanied by his friend Redman and two angry, gesticulating natives. Stuzyuiski's trousers were smeared to the knees with blood, and there were deep scratches on his hands. He had jumped into an open lobster pit belonging to the natives and been severely clawed for his efforts.

The shore patrol was back at nine-fifteen with Kalinka, the shipfitter. The charge was making an indecent proposal to an elderly lady. These two particular shore patrolmen had already been out several times, and they stopped now for a cup of coffee. They told Carney that this was the first Navy ship in Elysium in a month and that since eight o'clock they had put on ten extra shore patrolmen.

Ten minutes after they left, two other shore patrolmen came aboard and announced that Schlemmer, the signalman, was being held by the local police on a charge of rape.

At nine-forty-five or thereabouts, three M.P.'s drove up with Denowsky, Corcoran, and Youngquist, all second division men, in tow. Denowsky, with the other two as riders, had stolen a D-8 bulldozer from an Army parking field and had knocked over three privies behind a barracks before being interfered with. The M.P.'s were pretty surly. Carney put another yellow slip in the log.

Five minutes later, Carney noticed a commotion back aft. A jacob's-ladder had been thrown over by number five hatch and a native girl was climbing it, assisted by Sam Insigna, the signalman, from the dock, and plenty of willing hands from the ship. Carney had to interfere, and Sam led the girl off. The two kept looking back at the ship. Carney wiped his brow groggily.

It was only a few blocks from the dock to the center of town. Shortly after ten o'clock, Carney heard a big noise over in town. There was a great deal of shouting and some screaming. This went on for maybe ten minutes and then there was the sound of at least three sirens. The noise stopped a few minutes later. Ten minutes after, an M.P. command truck and a shore patrol paddy wagon pulled up on the dock. Both were loaded to the brim with members of the starboard section. These men were a gory sight. Almost all of them were covered with blood and dripping blood. Their uniforms were in tatters and a few had lost their trousers. Vanessi, the storekeeper, had at least four teeth missing and several men had what appeared to be burns. Carney turned them over to the Doctor. They all seemed perfectly happy, those who were up and about. Even those who were unconscious had a peaceful smile on their faces. The shore patrol spoke ill-naturedly of a big fight with some soldiers in a dance hall. The shore patrol looked tired.

It took half an hour to put that bunch away. Then the Doctor went along number three hatch examining the bodies with a flashlight. The hatch cover was getting crowded.

At eleven-thirty, just when Carney was thinking he might get through the watch without further incident, a Navy station wagon stopped at the gangway. Four shore patrolmen got out, two officers and two enlisted men. The enlisted men, wearing forty-fives, stationed themselves at the foot of the gangway. The officers came on up. The Commander of the Naval Base, they said, had ordered the sentries stationed to prevent anyone, officer or man, from leaving the ship during the rest of its stay in Elysium. The immediate reason was that some sailors, certainly members of this crew, had broken into the home of the French consul and thoroughly taken it apart. Carney nodded dumbly. By this time he was well beyond surprise.

As they turned to go, one of the officers asked: 'How long since these guys made a liberty, anyway?' Carney told him. The officer shook his head wearily and went on down the gangway.

That was all then. Pauley, who had the mid-watch,

had an easy time. A few more bodies were brought aboard, and at two o'clock one of the bodies already laid out revived and tried to slide down the bow spring line. Those were the only incidents. Otherwise peace settled soddenly on the *Reluctant*. The liberty was over.

With the matin clarity of the new day, certain significant details of the liberty were revealed. The members of the starboard section were coherent this morning, although not inclined to be talkative, and from their information it was possible to reconstruct the evening. Upon leaving the ship, the entire section had repaired to the local saloons, where it spent the afternoon and early evening drinking native gin and cane whiskey. According to the reports, well corroborated by the evidence on top of number three, these were sturdy and mature drinks. By nine o'clock they had mowed down half of the starboard section. The main body of the survivors, about twenty strong, had marched upon a USO dance given for the Army. They were made to feel unwelcome there. The fight, while short, was intense. A few of the hostesses got caught in the middle of things and lost much of their clothing. The Chinese lanterns burning overhead were pulled down and accounted for numerous first-degree burns. The *Reluctant* contingent, outnumbered three to one, was at least holding its own when the M.P.'s arrived.

In addition to this main force there were several diversionary groups. Although no one would admit to direct knowledge of this, it was conceded that perhaps one small group had visited the home of the French consul. The rumor was that a whimsical taxi-driver had advertised it as a whore-house. The visitors were justifiably angry when they found no girls in the darkened house, and among one of the several demonstrations of righteous wrath had thrown a large world globe through the living-room window.

A few other small patrols, such as those of Costello and Denowsky, had fanned to the outskirts of the town and found employment there. This, in outline, completed the picture of the evening.

The big news, though, was that David Bookser had not returned from liberty. This news startled everyone. A few of the crew remembered having seen him walking forlornly about town in the early afternoon, but no one recalled seeing him after three o'clock. It is interesting that the unanimous verdict of officers and crew was that Bookser had somehow met with foul play. It wasn't even considered that he might simply be over-leave. The exec sent Ensign Keith (escorted by the wary shore patrol) over to the Naval Base Commander to request a search for Bookser.

The *Reluctant* was three more days in Elysium. It was a time of healing and of aftermath. Schlemmer was released from jail when Ensign Keith went over and paid his fine. He was released because his complainant, a young lady of considerable professional reputation, could not be found to press charges. On the second day the Captain was summoned to the Base Commander's office. Afterward it was joyously circulated that he had gotten a royal ass-eating, and it was proudly reported that the Base Commander had informed him the ship would never be permitted to return to Elysium. On the third day two hundred dollars was withdrawn from the welfare fund and paid to a native truck farmer as reparation for one cow, deceased.

And still there was no trace of Bookser. The crew was visibly disturbed about this. Most still thought that Bookser had met with foul play — 'one of them Army bastards.' A few more argued that Bookser had just gone over the hill — 'a religious kid like that, you know, he probably just got fed up.' Two or three advanced theorists thought that Bookser had been stricken with something like amnesia. All were sorry that he was gone. When they talked of him now, it was in an elegiac way. 'He was a good kid,' they would say, using the past tense.

Except for the shadow that Bookser cast, the entire membership of the crew was in good spirits. The officers wondered about this. There was certainly ample cause for the port section to feel deadly enmity toward the starboard section; and yet an atmosphere of abnormal friendliness prevailed. On the last night in Elysium the reason for this good fellowship was made clear.

Wiley, the gunner's mate, came up to Mr. Langston, the O.O.D., and asked if it was true that the ship was sailing in the morning. Mr. Langston said it was. Wiley scratched his head and said, 'Well, in that case I guess we better . . .' He leaned over and talked low into

Langston's ear. Mr. Langston almost jumped. 'Holy Christ, yes!' he croaked. 'Get her off of here!' Wiley scampered below and returned a moment later leading a bewildered-looking native girl by the hand. The girl was dark and squat and rather ugly, and she wore sandals and a very dirty white cotton dress. She looked tired. 'This is Malina,' said Wiley, as he led her past the gaping Langston and on down the gangway. 'Thanks!' he said to Langston as he bounded aboard again.

Langston had recovered a little and asked: 'How did she get aboard?'

Wiley said easily: 'Oh, Sam Insigna brought her out that first night. He tried to get her up a ladder on this side, but Mr. Carney seen him, so Sam got a bumboat and brought her out to the other side.'

'Where in *hell* did you keep her?' Langston said.

'Down in hawser stowage. They fixed it up nice for her down there.' Wiley grinned, and added an afterthought: 'She liked it on here. She made four hundred some bucks!'

The ship sailed next morning at ten. At breakfast time even those who had held out hope gave Bookser up for lost. He came back at nine-thirty. The deck divisions were standing by to handle lines, and the second division was assembling to hoist up the gangway. The quartermasters were gathering on the bridge and the signalmen on the flying bridge. A majority of the crew was witness to the manner of Bookser's return.

An American-make car drove along the docks; a girl driving, a sailor with her. The car turned into the entrance to a warehouse, a little distance from the gangway, and stopped. Perhaps the two in the car thought they couldn't be seen there. They could: they were. The men on deck watched, and the signalmen on the bridge watched, and after a moment the signalmen watched with binoculars. And this is what they all saw:

They saw this girl. With the naked eye the men on deck could see that she was pretty. With the glasses, the signalmen saw that she was beautiful. Her skin was burnished gold and her hair a black, glistening shawl about her shoulders. Her forehead was high and proud and her eyes were blue. The signalmen could see the tears in her eyes as she turned to the sailor, Bookser. Bookser kissed the girl and stroked back her lovely hair; and the deckhands watched and the signalmen watched. The kiss grew and lengthened and tightened and became the embrace of farewell; and the hands of the two ran helplessly down each other's bodies; and these hands told everything to the signalmen with the 7-50 binoculars. Then Bookser got out and the car drove away.

When Bookser came aboard and started forward to the compartment, the men on deck swarmed about him. They closed in with noisy cries and on their lips were eager, impatient questions. And then they stopped. There was something about Bookser that silenced them, something strange and high and inaccessible. He was pale and listless, and in his eyes there was sadness, and something worlds far away. 'Hello,' he said quietly, and he gave a little crooked smile. And the crew was suddenly humble before him. The coarse, impatient questions died on their lips and in their place came reverent, hesitant ones.

'Were you with her all the time, Booksie?'

Bookser nodded wearily.

'Where did you meet her, Booksie?'

'Over in the church,' Booker said vaguely.

'Who does she live with?'

'She lives alone up on top of the hill.'

'What was her name, Booksie?'

'Lenora. Lenora Valencia.'

'How did you know to come back before we sailed?'

'Her uncle,' Booker said dully. 'Her uncle is foreman of the stevedores here.'

And then, as Booker turned to go, Steuben, the yeoman, asked the necessary, inevitable question. He asked it with infinite respect.

'Booksie, were you shacked up with her?'

There was a little silent moment. Booker looked at them, and there was pride in his eyes, and defiance, and this awful loneliness. He nodded slowly. Then, slowly, he went down to the compartment.

The ship sailed then. It was a blue, shiny morning and a spanking off-shore breeze corrugated the surface and streaked its vivid blue with white. The *Reluctant* steamed along the coastwise channel, and the breeze pushed staunchly against the starboard bow. Elysium slipped astern, receded, diminished in scale against the dome of the sky. The fresh breeze blew on the faces of the crew lined along the rails, and they felt good. They were leaving Elysium, the only civilization the ship had known in three years; they were going back to obscene waters and steaming islands and sweating days and nights, and still they felt good. They felt good in the same way that an old and happy couple feels good, or that soldiers feel good after a battle, or that any group with the bright bond of communal achievement feels good. The crew was a unit at last, and the common artery of participation ran through and bound together such distant and diverse characters as Costello and Wiley and Ringgold and Schlemmer. They stood along the rail in little groups; but these were accidental groups with interchangeable membership, and not the tight, jealous cliques of old. Stuzyuiski and Kalinka, the shipfitter, who hadn't spoken to each other in a year, stood and kidded together. The crew felt good: they had a good thing under their belts, a cherished package waiting to be opened, a prize awaiting distribution.

When Elysium was small in the distance and without detail, like something seen through the wrong end of a pair of binoculars, they opened the package. Each group opened it at about the same time, and each opened it the same way: slowly, gently, lovingly.

One man would open his corner of it:

'Did you see me clip that big sergeant at the dance? One of them gals had her blouse torn and one of her tits hanging out, and he was gawking at her, and I stepped up and caught him right on the button!'

And another would open it a little more:

'Yeah, and did you see me! I was standing up by the bandstand and this soldier takes a dive at me and I seen him coming and stepped out of the way and he went right on through that big goddamn drum!'

And a port section man would open his corner:

'You know that gal Insigna kept down in number two? Did you know she got loose one night and started wandering around and she was just heading into officers' country when they caught her!'

And finally, and proudly, the real heart of the package, the prize, the essence, was exposed:

'But did you hear about Bookser! That crazy little son-of-a-gun went over there all by himself and got shacked up with the most beautiful gal you ever saw! The signalmen said she was absolutely beautiful! They say he met her in a church over there — a church, for Christ's sake! And she kept him up at her house and he stayed over-leave and she brought him back just in time to catch the ship! Bookser, for Christ's sake!'

These things are quite symphonic in their development. Now, at first, the theme was stated simply and quietly. Later on, at chow, in the compartment, on the crawling night watches, it would be embellished and enlarged. Then various contrapuntal themes would be introduced: one man would add something new and isolated that happened, and another would insert something that didn't happen, but should have. That way the thing would grow and take shape, and finally, when it was rich and rounded and complete, it would sum-

marily be scrapped and a new structure begun from
the same material. There was plenty of material: the
crew had struck a rich vein at Elysium. It was one
which would build them a wall of strength against the
attack of buttressed miserable days and nights.

And while the crew stood examining this rich thing,
the solitary figure of David Bookser emerged from the
compartment hatchway. Bookser had changed to dungarees, and now for a moment he stood blinking in the
sunlight. It might have been a cue, the way all eyes
turned to him. With the slow, mechanical step of a
sleepwalker he started up the fo'c'sle. The groups broke
and made way for him. They smiled at him and called
to him: they spoke with warm and friendly but respectful voices, the way they might address a beloved officer
like Mr. Roberts. Several men sitting on bitts got up
and offered their seats to Bookser. But Bookser just
smiled a sad, vague smile and nodded his head and
kept going. He walked up to the very prow, and he
stood there and turned his head back toward the pin-
point cluster of Elysium and didn't move.

The crew stayed on deck for quite a while, until the
islands began to grow dubious on the horizon. Then
one by one, and in twos and threes, they went below:
to work, to sleep, to sit and talk. Finally Bookser alone
was left. He stood in the prow like a statue. Then,
when the line of the islands was finally gone from the
sky, he too went below. He went down to take among
the crew his rightful place as hero-elect of a legend
in the making.

LIEUTENANT ROBERTS was the only one on the ship who gave a damn about the war in Europe, and he cared profoundly. Scarcely anybody else even listened to the news, much less absorbed it. And it was a time of great news. Now, in the last days of April and the first days

of May, 1945, the Third Reich lay in its death throes.
Peace for much of the world was only days away, maybe hours. It had already been rumored and denied,
rumored and denied again. It was a time as exciting
and, in the best sense, as great as the world had ever
known: and in its minute displacement of the Pacific
Ocean, the *Reluctant* went about its business and
didn't even look up. Its talk was of worn and familiar
things: the States, the chow in the messhall, the movies,
the recent trip to Elysium, and long and always, the
Captain. Once in a while a man would ask another,
'They still fighting over there in Europe?' but he did it
only to display his global awareness. He didn't really
care.

Germany writhed in the awful constriction of Allied
and Russian armies, vomited agony. The last-ditch de-
fenders fought from the sewers of Berlin. Lieutenant
Roberts sat for hours at a time in the radio shack with
a headset on his ears, listening to the fading, crackling
voices of the shortwave broadcasts. It was seldom that
the ship was at an island owning a radio station, and
much of the time shortwave was the only means of
getting the news. The phonograph in the wardroom,
endlessly tended by Carney or Billings or Langston,
endlessly whining the sick, scratchy, distorted love-
songs of two years ago — 'I'll Never Smile Again,' 'You'll
Never Know,' 'Wrong, Would It Be Wrong to Care' —
drove Roberts to the headset in the radio shack. It was
virtually impossible to silence the monotone nostalgia
of the turntable long enough for a news broadcast.

Once Roberts had persuaded Billings, the communicator, to put out every morning a sheet of mimeographed press news. The experiment lasted only a week, and even Roberts had to admit its failure. The copies were being tossed unread into the trash baskets.

Roberts had just had a run-in with the Captain when the news came of the final surrender of Germany. The *Reluctant* lay at anchor in the bay of one of the islands. It was early evening when the word came, the four-to-eight watch; and Roberts had the watch. Because there was no gangway down, he stood it on the bridge. There were several difficulties with the Captain. First the quartermaster dropped a megaphone on the deck of the wheelhouse, and the Captain was heard from on that. His cabin was directly below, and he couldn't stand noise overhead of any sort. At night, awakening him from sleep, an object dropped on the deck overhead would send him nearly out of his mind with rage.

Then, after the first incident, it wasn't ten minutes until the Captain came up on the bridge again. He was obviously looking for trouble, and he found it. He saw a group of men on the foredeck leaning on the rail. Leaning on the rail was his currently favorite prohibition. He stormed over to Lieutenant Roberts on the wing.

'Do you see those men down there?' he demanded.

Roberts looked up with the minor annoyance of a man brushing away a fly. He nodded complacently.

'Well!' shouted the Captain. 'What're you going to do about it?'

Roberts looked around indifferently and summoned the messenger. 'Go down and tell those men to get off the rail,' he said casually.

The Captain's mustache bristled. His face and neck got red. 'Get off the rail, nothing!' he shouted. 'You get their names and, by God, you put them on report. You get those men on report in a goddamn quick hurry or, by God, I'll take care of you!' He started muttering then and walking agitatedly about. He never was a match for Roberts and he knew it.

Roberts turned wearily to the messenger. 'Go down and get their names,' he said. The way he said it, it was understood that they were humoring a foolish child. Then he turned and walked away to the other wing, leaving the Captain muttering a familiar monologue: 'By God, what do you think I make these orders for — just to be doing something? By God, when I say something's going to be done, it's going to be done, or, by God, I'll take care of you officers! Bet your ass I will . . .' A few minutes later, when Thompson, the radioman, came out and told Roberts that Germany had just surrendered unconditionally, he forgot all about the Captain.

As soon as he was relieved, Roberts went into the radio shack and put on the headset. The air was full of the great news. Roberts heard a transcription of the rolling eloquence of Churchill. He heard the text of the President's proclamation from Washington. He heard the quiet, controlled exultation of General Eisenhower. He heard the news commentators. They talked from

Reims, from 'somewhere in Germany,' from Paris, from Rome, from Lisbon, from London. They told of the celebration in their cities on this, a day of such triumph as the world had never known. There were splendid fireworks in Paris over the Place de l'Opéra. There were snake dances through the streets of Rome. In London, the pubs were jammed and the streets were jammed. Flags and bunting instantaneously bloomed from the buildings, and there were parades of crack Guard regiments. In New York, Times Square, of course, was thronged. Ticker-tape rained from Wall Street windows. The universal joy was only feebly relieved by cognizance of the still unwon Pacific war.

Roberts sat for a long time at the headset: it must have been two hours that he listened. When one station went off the air, he switched to another. Almost frantically he would seek out a new station. Finally the news programs were all off the air, or repeating themselves. Finally there were only the sad iterations of American dance music on the radio bands. Roberts got up then.

The movie was just letting out. There were sudden shouts in the passageways, and the loud, happy voices of the crew as they swarmed forward to the fo'c'sle. It must have been a good movie. Hearing them, Roberts felt a sudden loneliness. He felt a vague sorrow and, pressing just behind it, an awful sick despair that he had lived with for a long, familiar time. He needed suddenly to talk to someone. He needed to tell them the news, and he needed, in return, some strange assurance; and this was not understood. He went down to the wardroom.

Carney and Billings were alone in there. They pored over their acey-deucey game. The phonograph played 'Paper Doll.' There was a crack in the record that clicked at every turn. The big fan droned in the corner.

Roberts stood over them for a moment. 'The war's over in Europe,' he said. 'Germany has surrendered.' He stood waiting.

Carney looked up politely. 'Yeah?' he said. Then, evidently feeling that some amplifying comment was indicated, he added: 'Well, that ought to speed things up out here a good bit.'

'Yeah,' said Billings, 'it should.' He picked up the dice.

'What's the name of the game?' he asked.

'Acey-deucey,' said Carney.

'Acey-deucey,' said Billings. He rolled the dice. 'There it is.'

Roberts smiled a little and went out. He should have known better than to expect anything else. No one could help him because no one gave a hoot in hell what went on beyond the confines of this ship. It was to the rest of the officers a matter of indifference that a war of supreme horror had ended. Just to establish this, Roberts went around and told his friends the news. Lying in bed reading a year-old Street and Smith detective magazine, Ed Pauley agreed substantially with Carney: 'Well, maybe they'll get on the ball out here now.' Ensign Pulver was languidly militant: 'I guess we took care of the bastards good this time!' Ensign Moulton was cynical: 'That'll hold them for another twenty years.' Ensign Keith wanted to know, did they catch Hitler? Finally Roberts went to the Doc's room. If anyone could help, it would be the Doc.

The Doctor was reading at his desk. The desk light shone on his forehead and on the bald part of his head. Without seeming to shift his eyes, he shot a quick, sharp glance at the doorway. 'Come in!' he called to Roberts. He put the book aside.

'Sit down. Take a load off.'

'Hi, Doc,' said Roberts. He sat down in the chair beside the desk, locked his hands behind his head, and leaned back against the bulkhead. 'The war is over in Europe. Germany surrendered unconditionally at Reims.'

The Doctor stroked his mustache thoughtfully. 'That's fine,' he said. 'That's really splendid news. Has it been announced from Washington?'

Roberts nodded.

'That's very wonderful news,' said the Doc softly. 'Very wonderful.'

Roberts kept his hands locked behind his head. 'Doc, here's something for you,' he said slowly. 'The most horrible war in history has just ended. A terrible war, Doc, a truly terrible one. You would expect this, then, to be a time of the wildest general rejoicing. And what do I feel? — Doc, I feel depressed as all hell. What do you make of that?'

The Doctor squinted his eyes and leaned back in his

chair. 'Well,' he said, 'I shouldn't think that so remark-able. With anything as consummately absorbing as a great war there's always a great deal of transference. You know: the great general conflict swallows the little individual conflicts. Also there's the matter of war considered as a spectacle. War is a hell of a hypnotic and buoyant thing — viewed from a distance, a considerable distance — and it's quite reasonable to expect a letdown when it ends.'

Roberts shook his head and smiled. 'No,' he said. 'It's not like that at all. I guess I'm just being ingratiating in asking, because I know what it is. So do you. It's just that I feel left out. I wanted in that war, Doc. I wanted in it like hell. Does that sound stupid?'

'No,' said the Doc, 'but it is rare.' He lighted a cigarette. 'You never did satisfactorily explain to me how come you're so all-fired anxious to fight this war.'

'I don't know that I could,' said Roberts. 'I don't know how you go about explaining a compulsion. That's what it is, of course.'

Roberts had a crooked smile. 'Did I ever tell you,' he went on, 'what a long and consistent record I have as a frustrated anti-fascist?'

The Doctor shook his head and exhaled smoke. 'I think you omitted that.'

'Well, I have,' said Roberts. 'A truly distinguished record of frustration. When I was eighteen I quit high school and went to New York and got signed up as an ambulance driver in the Lincoln Brigade. That time the war was over before they could ship me out.' He scratched his ear. 'But I guess there wasn't much anti-fascism to that. It was just a hell of a gaudy thing to do. I was quite a hero when I left.'

'Then,' he went on, 'in 1940, in my last year of pre-med, I quit school again. This time I went up to Montreal and tried to get in the RAF. I think by then I honestly had an idea of what was involved. It was strictly nothing doing, though' — he tapped his teeth — 'they threw me out on this foolish malocclusion. Same thing in 1941 when I tried to get in the Air Corps — all three of them. They wouldn't have anything to do with me. This is the only outfit that would have me.'

The Doc looked thoughtfully at Roberts. 'You give this war a lot, don't you?'

'Yes, I do,' said Roberts. 'But you don't.'

'No,' the Doc agreed. 'I don't. I see it as a war of unrelieved necessity — nothing more. Any ideology attaching is only incidental. Not to say accidental.'

'Well,' said Roberts, 'no need for us to go into that again. But Doc, if you had asked me four years ago I could have told you to hell and back what this war was about. I would have overwhelmed you with moral superiority. I would have used terms like "war against fascism," "holy war," "crusade," and so forth. I would have defined fascism as a revolution against the human soul, and I would have talked of the forces of good and evil. And perhaps, Doc, there was a lot of justice in that sort of talk. Perhaps there still is: I don't know. It seems to me that causes are hellishly elusive things, and that the moment you try to articulate them, give them a label, they shy away and become something else. I don't know, Doc.'

He paused. 'I guess the minimum thing I'd say now is that the war seems to me — or should I say seemed — immensely worth while (positively and consciously and inherently, that is — not accidentally, as you say), and that I feel a hell of a compulsion to be in it.' He held up his hands quizzically and looked at the Doctor.

The Doc was quiet a moment; then he said: 'I could kick your ass for ever leaving med school.'

'So could I,' said Roberts. 'Now. Particularly now. Particularly today. I chase the hell out of this war and it quits on me.'

'I would remind you that there is still a war out here which you may very well see plenty of.'

Roberts shook his head. 'Not a chance. I've sat on this bucket this long. I'll sit here now till it's over.'

'And I would further remind you,' said the Doc, 'that it's through no fault of yours that you're on this bucket instead of in a grave in Germany.'

Roberts grinned. 'What an enchanting thought!' he said.

The Doctor pushed back from the desk. 'And I would still further remind you,' he said briskly, 'that what we need is a drink. How about getting the orange juice?'

'You're right,' said Roberts. He went and got the orange juice and the Doc broke out the alcohol and they sat together with their drinks for over an hour. The Doc was at his best. He told some splendid stories. He told about the fairy patient of his who had tried to

change his sex with a self-amputation. He told a couple
of fine stories about alcoholics. When he left an hour
later, Roberts felt some better. The Doc's company had
smothered a little of his depression. He thought now
that perhaps he could sleep: it was after eleven. He
went up and turned in.

But he couldn't sleep. Langston snored lustily in the
top bunk, and he lay and studied the lights of the
island circled in the porthole. At first he tried to keep
his thoughts centered on neutral, tranquil things; but
soon, like a car with a locked steering-gear, they ran
helplessly out of control and he was back again with
his old conflict, and thinking again of the war and the
victory. He was thinking now of the celebrating cities,
of the celebrating cities that had known the war. There
were snake dances through the streets of Rome, they
said. He tried to see Rome, but he couldn't make it
convincing. Paris was easier: he could see the fireworks
over the massed roofs of Paris and the crowds surging
along the Champs d'Elysées and upsetting chairs and
tables in the boulevard cafés. Surely they would upset
the chairs and tables. London he could see very well:
the parading regiments and the intimately cheering
crowds and the grinning soldiers and the officers weav-
ing just a little as they marched at the head of their
companies. The pubs would be absolute madhouses
and the beer would be passed back over the heads of
the mob to be spilled or drunk before it ever got beyond
the third row, and everybody would laugh and nobody
gave a damn, and way at the back someone would

shout despairingly for his beer. Naked girls would appear at the balcony windows of hotel rooms and call happy things down to the streets, and then an arm would appear and drag them laughing and squealing back into the room. It would be like that in all the cities that had a stake in this day; pushing, shouting, laughing, fighting, drinking, lovemaking; all personal identities frenziedly submerged in the shining common identity of a fabulous victory.

Roberts saw all these things in separate scenes, as though they were the changing slides of a stereoscope. And now, suddenly, the series of the tumultuous cities clicked out and in its place came a very different scene. It was a scene Roberts recognized from its origin as a picture in *Life* magazine. (My knowledge of the war comes straight from *Life*, he thought ironically.) There was a field in France, and a farmer was harrowing this field, walking behind the harrow. The furrowed rows were very straight, except in the middle of the field, where they broke and gave way for the mounded grave of a British Tommy. It looked like lovely country, green with trees, with the soft haze of distant hills in the background. The rows of the harrow detoured for just the area of the grave and then they ran on straight and unswerving. It was that way the war, too, had moved off and left the Tommy. The grave looked lonely in the bright sunshine.

The dead, Roberts mused, what could you say for the dead of this war? What could you *really* say? Well, there were a lot of things you could say automatically and without thought, but they were all the wrong things; and just this once, just this one war, anyhow, let us try to say true things about the dead. Begin by cancelling the phrase, 'our honored dead': for that is not true — we forget them, we do not honor them but in rhetoric — and the phrase is the badge of those who want something of the dead. If the dead of this war must have a mutual encomium, then let it be 'poor dead bastards.' There is at least a little humanity in that. And let us not say of them, this time, 'they gave their lives' for something or other; for certainly there was nothing voluntary in their dying. And neither is it fair to speak of 'dead heroes,' for not at all necessarily does the fact of death include the fact of heroism. Some of these dead were shining youths scornful of the sanctity of their own lives, who lived daily with terror rarefied by inevitability and died with a flawless gesture of self-immolation: and others died as the result of injuries sustained in falling through a privy. But, thought Roberts, if they did not live equally, they are every one equally dead; and you could say this affirmative thing of all: that in a war of terrifying consequence and overwhelming agony, they participated one hundred per cent. That was the only true thing you could say for all, but it was enough. The war demanded the shortening of how many — two million, five hundred and sixty thousand, two hundred and fourteen? — lives, and these men were chosen. So pile them high at Austerlitz and Waterloo and Ypres and Verdun, and add a few new places, Aachen and Dunkerque and Anzio; only do not talk lies about the dead. They are the chosen.

Chosen? thought Roberts. Was that the right word?
Perhaps it was. Perhaps it was *just* the word. Maybe
there was some gigantic over-all selection that named
the men good enough to fight the war and consigned to
ships like this the ones who weren't. Perhaps they were
all, on here, something less than men in a war that demanded men; subtly deficient in a war that required
completeness. Take the Captain; what could be more
blatant than his inadequacy? Maybe it was that way
with all of them — with Ed Pauley and Carney and
Billings and Keith and himself — and all the others.
Perhaps it was that in some infallible system of measur-
ing men they fell short: some incompetency in the
nerve endings, the white corpuscles, the adrenal gland;
the stamina of their mother, the integrity of great-
great-great-grandfather; the shape of their remem-
brance of first-known fear; something . . .

Sleep was out of the question. Roberts sat up suddenly, rubbed his eyes. Langston snored above him in
a perfect monotone. He got up, and in the dark put on
his clothes. He bumped against the coaster chair and
made a noise, but there was no hitch in Langston's
breathing. Roberts went out and down the ladder to
the quarterdeck. It was a cool night with a little breeze
blowing, and overhead there were patches of clouds.
Over on the island the lights burned their night vigil,
and now and then a jeep or a truck went by along the
beach road. Tonight, perhaps because it was a cool
night for sleeping, there were no late-talking groups
sitting about on the deck. Roberts couldn't see another

soul on deck. He started walking up and down on the quarterdeck.

V-E day aboard the *Reluctant,* he composed, was observed quietly, without ostentatious display, and with a grim awareness of the still unfinished Pacific war. Appropriately, the ship's company marked the great day in restrained but distinctive fashion. Lieutenant Carney and Lieutenant (jg) Billings, swept up in the spirit of the moment, played a game of acey-deucey in the wardroom. Lieutenant (jg) Pauley celebrated with quiet taste by reading a detective magazine. Lieutenant (jg) Langston observed the day by retiring at nine instead of ten, and by sleeping a little more soundly than usual. Ensign Pulver was moved to the extent of rigging a new portable fan at the foot of his bunk. The gruff but lovable Captain couldn't quite conceal an unusual generousness of spirit, placing only twelve men on report during a fifteen-minute period. But in these small though significant ways it was, for the *Reluctant,* just another work day on the road to Tokyo . . .

And all of a sudden Roberts had to do something. And it had to be against the Captain: it had to be. This thing was suddenly just as obligatory and inevitable as his next breath; and just the thought of it was like a door opening out of prison. And he knew right away what to do. The Captain's palm tree. The Captain kept a small palm tree in a painted five-gallon can on the wing of his bridge, and it was the joy of his life. With slow, deadly certainty Roberts walked up to the boat deck and out on the Captain's wing. There, in the corner, was the palm tree. It was very dark and he couldn't hear anyone moving about on the bridge overhead. He jerked the palm out by the roots and threw it over the side. Then he took the can and scattered the loose earth about on the deck. Then he put the can down and went around aft of the house. Already he felt worlds better, but still there was something undone. And immediately that thing was revealed to him too.

Automatically he recalled the Captain's obsessional hatred of noise, particularly noise at night, particularly noise in the area of his cabin. He went down to the cabin deck and found what he wanted. It was a gangway stanchion, about the size of a baseball bat, and solid lead. He went up to the port wing of the Captain's bridge and calculated. The Captain's bedroom was just inside, and the Captain slept athwartships. The head of his bunk was right against this bulkhead. Roberts figured: it was about three feet off the deck; it was right about here. He swung the stanchion with all his strength against the bulkhead. Then he swung a second time and a third. The blows shook the house like an explosion. Next morning every single officer confessed to having been awakened, and Ensign Moulton, who lived just aft of the Captain, said he had been knocked almost out of his bunk. Roberts placed the stanchion carefully at the Captain's door, walked calmly down the ladder and around the house, and returned to his own room by the starboard ladder. He undressed carefully and got into bed.

Langston was awake and sitting dazedly up. 'What the hell was that noise?' he mumbled.

Roberts pulled the sheet up to his chin. 'I didn't hear any noise,' he said. And then he added, 'But I do now.' He could hear the screaming voice of the Captain, and the opening of doors, and the scurrying of many feet, as of quartermasters and messengers running down from the bridge. They were wonderfully pleasant noises. Roberts listened to them for several minutes, until he fell soundly asleep.

T HE CAPTAIN'S PALM TREE must have held for him a symbolism or complex sentimental value far exceeding that of its eye appeal, which was negligible. It must have, else how could you account for his reaction to its sabotage? The Captain's reaction was violent. It was roughly ten minutes past eight in the morning when he stepped out on the wing of his boat deck and discovered the loss. Immediately he let out a bellow for poor little Cornwall, his steward's mate. He pointed fiercely at the loose earth strewn about the empty overturned five-gallon can. 'Don't touch that!' he shouted at the bewildered Cornwall. 'Don't let anybody near that!' It is hard to say just what his purpose might have been: perhaps in the first minutes of his grief and righteous wrath the Captain thought to make a shrine of the scene of vandalism. At any rate, later in the day he made Cornwall sweep up the mess.

Then the Captain bounded up the ladder to the bridge. His face was stained deep purple as he lurched toward the microphone of the P.A. system. He had a moment of furious trouble with the switches and buttons, and then his amplified and unmistakable voice startled the morning peace.

Awakening was for the crew of the *Reluctant* an unusually gradual process. It began feebly at six-thirty when Chief Johnson held reveille. It continued at seven when a majority of the crew actually got up and began to move dazedly about. Usually it was ten o'clock or thereabouts when the process was completed. The Captain materially speeded things up this morning. His voice came to the crew like a douse of ice water:

'All right now, goddamit, listen to this. Some smart son-of-a-bitch has been up here and thrown my palm tree over the side, and last night he was getting smart and pounding on my bulkhead. Now I'm telling you, by God, right here and now I'm going to find out who done that if I have to tear this ship upside-down doing it. By God, I'll do that if I have to! Bet your ass! There's going to be a general court-martial for the fellow who did that! Now if you know anyone who had anything to do with it, you better get up here and tell me. That's your duty, by God, that's your duty. I can tell you right here and now that there won't be any liberty on board of this here ship until I find the son-of-a-bitch who's been getting so goddamn smart!'

This was substantially the text of the Captain's address. The delivered version was actually longer, but then it tended toward repetition and, in the end, incoherence. The crew listened at first with shock, then with wonder, and finally with conspicuous joy. 'Hey, did ya hear that?' they shouted at one another. 'Somebody threw the Old Man's tree over the side!' All of a sudden it was a wonderful day, and every man on the ship was instantaneously wide awake. Down in the compartment men guffawed and slapped each other on the back. There was less evident rejoicing out on deck, under the Captain's eye, but it was there just the same. The threat of restriction depressed no one, for this was a crew of realists, all of whom knew that the ship wasn't going anywhere near another liberty port after Elysium. It would have been hard to give them anything nicer than the Captain's news.

After addressing the crew, the Captain summoned Mr. LeSueur, the executive officer, and addressed him for fifteen minutes. The pitch and volume of Captain's voice were high. It was reported he told Mr. LeSueur that if he didn't find who threw his tree over the side and pounded on his bulkhead, by God, he'd put him, Mr. LeSueur, in hack for ten days! Bet your ass! He ordered Mr. LeSueur to send a boat ashore to dig up *two* small palm trees and return with them. He further ordered Mr. LeSueur to set a watch on the starboard wing of the boat deck from sunset until 8 A.M. The sole duty of the watch would be to guard the two palm trees, and God help them if they went to sleep!

The Captain had a busy morning. After Mr. LeSueur he summoned and received a series of visitors. It was shrewdly noted that they were the very crew members consistently civil to him. Undoubtedly the Captain reasoned that civility constituted loyalty, and that these were his friends. All of these visitors reported the same thing: that he had tried to pump them for information. All of them told that the Old Man had cocked his head and coyly assured them that he had a damn good idea who it was and that, by God, he'd fix him. And all of them agreed that the Captain hadn't the foggiest idea which one of his hundred-and-seventy-odd enemies had struck.

The Captain wasn't the only one who was curious. The entire ship's company was excited over this unrevealed hero in their midst. They were avid to locate him and do him honor. Little thoughtful groups gathered throughout the day, and among them every name on the ship's roster was carefully considered for motive and potentiality. The only man who was entirely free of suspicion was Whipple, the storekeeper, who lay in sick-bay with his broken leg hanging by weights and pulleys from the overhead. There was no agreement among the investigating groups, although certain names were mentioned more often than others. Dowdy's name was mentioned quite a bit, and so was Olson's. Schlemmer, the signalman, was one active candidate, and Dolan, the quartermaster, was another. These four were accused countless times during the day, but none of them, it was noted by the most perceptive, had the air of valorous achievement properly obtaining to the true culprit. Although there were several confessions, none were by credible people, and the crew was frankly baffled.

The really smart boys in the crew figured it must have been an officer. An officer, they reasoned, had both greater opportunity and larger motive. These speculators were, of course, getting warm, but they never really got hot. They mentioned Lieutenant Roberts as a possibility, but they deferred him to Ensign Pulver and Lieutenant (jg) Ed Pauley. This was done because both Pulver and Pauley had a history of fierce and vocal threats against the Captain. Roberts never wasted his time that way. The smart boys finally settled on Pulver as their man, chiefly because he was so disarmingly unconvincing in denying his guilt. Ensign Pulver was flattered pink at the charge, and until the real one stepped forward he was entirely willing to be the interim culprit. He found it very agreeable. He went around all day being disgustingly coy.

Dowdy and Olson and Stefanowski, the machinist's mate, met as usual that evening in the armory. They spent a very quiet, happy, and domestic time. For a long while they sat and digested the rich news of the Captain's misfortune. Then Dowdy and Olson settled down to an acey-deucy game and Stefanowski went over to the phonograph and played Gene Autry records. At midnight Dolan came in. He had just come off watch, and he had thoughtfully acquired some eggs from the galley on his way down. He got out the hotplate, got out the frying-pan, and put the eggs on.

Stefanowski looked up from his records. 'I hear you threw the Old Man's tree over the side,' he greeted.

'No, I didn't,' said Dolan. He had a thoughtful look as he watched the eggs. 'But I know who did,' he added quietly.

Both Dowdy and Olson looked up from their game. 'Yeah?' said Olson.

Dolan nodded slowly. 'Roberts did it,' he said. 'Mister Roberts. I was on the bridge and I heard this splash and I saw him. He was just taking his time.'

Dowdy and Olson and Stefanowski looked at each other. 'Well, I'll be damned,' said Dowdy. 'Are you kidding?'

Dolan was dead serious. 'No, I ain't kidding. I saw him.' He added fiercely, 'Now, goddamit, that's just between the four of us. I ain't told nobody. You go spreading that around and you'll get him in trouble.'

'Yeah,' agreed Dowdy, 'we'll have to keep it quiet.' He grinned suddenly and pushed back from the acey-deucy board. 'Old Roberts,' he said admiringly. 'That's all right! By God, you might of known he done it!'

Stefanowski smacked the workbench. 'You goddamn right! He must be the guy that pounded hell out of the Old Man's bulkhead too. Man, he done a good day's work!'

Dolan said: 'That is one good son-of-a-bitching officer. That really is.' He looked to the others for agreement.

Dowdy nodded with heavy authority. 'I know I ain't never seen a better one.' He turned to Olson. 'How about you, Tom?' Dowdy and Olson were the two old-time Navy men on the ship and the final authorities on matters naval.

'No, I ain't,' said Olson. 'I seen a lot of pricks, though.'

'Yeah, so have I,' said Dowdy. 'I've seen some awful pricks. And the funny thing is a lot of them were mustangs. Old enlisted men. I was with a first-class boatswain's mate once who was just a hell of a nice guy. Everybody liked him. Then they made him an officer and right away he became the biggest bastard you ever saw. Everyone hated his guts after that.'

'That's right,' Olson concurred. 'I guess it's easy to be a nice guy when you ain't got any authority.'

'We got a pretty good bunch of officers on here,' Stefanowski said. 'On the whole, I mean.'

Dowdy looked at him a little coldly. 'You know why,

don't you?' he said superiorly, and then he went on:
'Because they don't do anything, that's why. Because
they just sit on their asses and don't give a damn about
nothing. Hell, it's easy to be a nice guy that way, when
you ain't trying to do anything. It's when you got work
to be done, when you've got to turn to a bunch of guys,
that you can really tell a good officer. Old Roberts,' he
said; 'now there is really an officer. He gets out there
and turns to himself and he turns everyone else to and,
by God, they still like him. He's still a nice guy and
that's the test. Just because these other bastards lie in
their sacks and don't bother anybody, you say they're
all right. How the hell do you know?'

It was a strong rebuke, and Stefanowski felt it. 'Yeah,'
he said penitently, 'I guess that's right.'

'You goddamn right that's right!' Dowdy snapped.

Stefanowski was quiet for a decent moment. Then
he said: 'Well, all I say is, Roberts ought to have a
medal for what he did. That was sure a hell of a fine
job!'

'Hell, yes,' said Dolan. 'Any guy that would fix the
Old Man up like that ought to have a medal.'

There was a little quiet moment while Dowdy eyed
the other three strangely. Then he said with an air of
decision: 'All right, let's give him a medal.'

'What?' said Stefanowski.

'Let's give him a medal.'

'Where you going to get it?' Stefanowski asked doubtfully.

Dowdy said scathingly: 'You got a lathe down there
in the machine shop, haven't you?'

'Yeah,' said Stefanowski, and there was the dawn of excitement in his voice.

'And you got plenty of sheet brass, haven't you?'

Stefanowski got it now. 'Yeah,' he said excitedly. 'Hell, yes!'

'Well, all right!' Dowdy said triumphantly. 'What more do you want? . . .'

At four o'clock next afternoon, Lieutenant Roberts sat in his room talking with Lieutenant (jg) Langston, his roommate. It had been a busy day, unloading dry stores onto barges, and Roberts had been out on deck since six o'clock. He was very tired and he sat in the coaster chair and contemplated a shower while he half-listened to Langston describing a Texas snake-hunt. There was a knock on the jamb of the opened door and Dowdy and Olson and Dolan and Stefanowski stood in the passageway.

'Come in,' Roberts called. The four filed inside. Stefanowski was holding a small green box.

Dowdy spoke: 'Could we see you a minute, Mr. Roberts?' He looked significantly over at Langston.

Roberts smiled. 'Sure,' he said. And in answer to Dowdy's look: 'That's all right.'

Stefanowski passed the box to Dowdy. Dowdy shuffled a moment and looked again doubtfully at Langston. Then he went ahead. 'Well, Mr. Roberts, we just wanted to give you this.' He handed the box to Roberts.

Roberts looked puzzledly at the box. He looked at the four awkward, embarrassed men. Then, smiling quizzically, he opened the box.

It was a nice box, and it had been floored with cotton. On the cotton, very bright, lay a strange device. It was a medal cut of shining brass in the shape of a full-grown palm tree with overhanging fronds. Fastened at the back of the medal was a piece of gorgeous silk, blue and red and yellow, secured at the other end to a safety-pin clasp. The palm tree was embedded in a rectangular base, and words had been painstakingly cut with a drill press into this base. Lieutenant Roberts read the words:

ORDER OF THE PALM

TO LIEUT. D. A. ROBERTS, FOR ACTION AGAINST

THE ENEMY, ABOVE AND BEYOND THE CALL OF DUTY,

ON THE NIGHT OF 8 MAY 1945

Roberts looked at the medal for a long time. Then he smiled and passed the medal over to Langston.

'That's very nice,' he said to Dowdy, 'but I'm afraid you've got the wrong man.'

He and Dowdy looked deeply at each other, and Dowdy grinned. 'Yessir,' Dowdy said. 'We know that, Mr. Roberts, but we'd kind of like you to have it, anyhow, sir.'

The smile on Roberts's face was funny and tight. He pinched the bridge of his nose. 'All right,' he said, 'I'll keep it. Thanks very much, all of you.'

All four were grinning proudly. 'Oh, that's nothing,' Dowdy said. 'Stefanowski here made it down in the shop.'

'It's a fine job,' Roberts complimented.

'Yessir, we think it is,' Dowdy said. The four stood awkwardly in the door. 'Well . . .' said Dowdy. The four started out, and then Dolan turned in the doorway and blurted: 'There ain't nobody that knows anything about this but us, Mr. Roberts. About the medal, I mean. Stefanowski, he didn't let anybody see it while he was cutting it.'

'That's fine,' Roberts said, 'but it doesn't matter.' He wanted to say something else, something of appreciation, but before he could form the words the group was gone from the doorway.

'Now I've got a medal to show my grandchildren,' he said quietly to Langston.

Langston passed the medal back. 'Did you take care of the palm tree?' he asked curiously.

'I must have,' Roberts said softly; and he smiled again that funny twisted smile. He took the box in his hands, and looked at the medal and at the absurd ribbon, read again the words so painstakingly cut; and for the first time in perhaps fifteen years he felt like crying.

W HEN, COMING OFF THE FOUR-TO-EIGHT WATCH,
Bergstrom, the quartermaster, set out to find his friend,
Thompson, the radioman, he knew exactly where to go.
Thompson, he knew, would be sitting in the messhall
playing Monopoly. Nominally, at least, it was Monop-

oly, but it was a brand that the copyright owners would scarcely have recognized. Thompson and the rest of the faithful who sat down to play every night in port before the movies had renovated it startlingly. The way it was played in the messhall, the object was no longer to amass the most property, but rather to pull off the greatest fraud. Loaded dice, sleight-of-hand, irregular counting practices, and various other forms of collusion were injected into that normally pallid game, with the result that it became no longer a game, but a spectacle played to a noisy but appreciative gallery of after-chow loungers. No player ever went into the contest armed with less than five thousand dollars of play money borrowed from another set, and nobody ever won; the game always ended when it narrowed down to two contestants of equally astronomical and ill-gotten wealth. It was a good show, and the kibitzers would demonstrate appreciatively whenever a particularly inspired piece of larceny was exposed. Thompson, because he demonstrated a talent for the game that bordered on genius, was their favorite; and the consensus was that once Thompson got on the outside he would abruptly become one of the world's wealthiest men.

It was a matter of some importance Bergstrom wanted to see his friend about, having to do with borrowing a couple of dungaree shirts until the laundry came back. When he left the bridge, Bergstrom looked into the radio shack just to make sure that Thompson wasn't on watch, then he went infallibly on down to the messhall. But Thompson wasn't there. The game was going on and the kibitzers were gathered, but it was a half-hearted performance because Thompson wasn't there cheating monstrously and laughing his head off. Bergstrom was quite surprised. For a few moments he watched the game and then he set out to find his friend. He looked in the compartment, where Thompson lived in the bunk above him, and he looked in the heads and he looked out on deck. He finally found him in the yeoman's office.

Thompson and their other great friend, Braue, the yeoman, were alone in there. Neither was talking, and both were sitting looking thoughtfully at the deck. Thompson had a kind of stare in his eyes.

Bergstrom closed the door behind him. 'How come no game tonight?' he started, and then he saw that something was wrong. 'What's the trouble?' he asked more quietly.

Thompson kept his eyes fixed on the deck. 'This,' he said. He handed over a crumpled dispatch blank and explained wearily while Bergstrom read it: 'My kid died, drowned in the ocean. Eighteen months old. I never even saw her.'

Bergstrom read on: ' . . . FUNERAL SATURDAY PLEASE TRY TO COME ALL MY LOVE FRANCES.' He folded the paper and returned it. This was Wednesday. 'Jesus, I'm sorry, Frank,' he said.

Thompson nodded in heavy acknowledgment. He raised his eyes and looked out the open porthole. 'That son-of-a-bitch,' he said tonelessly, as though it were something he had already said many times tonight.

'What's the matter?' Bergstrom asked softly.

Thompson stared at him without seeming to comprehend. 'That dirty son-of-a-bitch,' he said again. Then, with an effort, he answered: 'The Old Man. This' — he tapped the dispatch in his pocket — 'came in this afternoon. I went down and asked the bastard for emergency leave to fly home. Nothing doing. "We're not giving any emergency leaves on this ship." I said, "Captain, this has been approved by Mr. Billings and the exec. They don't need me up in the shack and I could be back here in a week if necessary. Before the ship even leaves here." "Nothing doing," he says, "and that's final. I'm not giving any emergency leaves. Start it with one guy and they'll all be running up here."' Thompson ground his teeth together. 'That dirty miserable son-of-a-bitch,' he said with heavy stress.

Bergstrom shook his head. 'God, that is a filthy trick,' he said.

They sat quiet for a moment. Thompson was looking again at the deck.

'What did Mr. Roberts tell you?' Braue asked thoughtfully.

'He told me to go over on the big island tomorrow and see the Chaplain and the flag secretary.'

Braue nodded approval. 'That's right,' he said. 'Those Chaplains and those people over on the beach throw a lot of weight. They can go right over the Old Man's head and put you on a plane.'

Thompson shrugged his shoulders and didn't say anything.

'You're going, aren't you?' Bergstrom asked. 'You're going over, aren't you?'

Thompson nodded. 'Yeah,' he said heavily, 'I'm going over. I saw the exec.'

'Sure,' said Bergstrom. 'There's a lot of planes going out of there. Chances are they can put you right on.'

Thompson kept his eyes fixed on the deck. He didn't say anything. After a moment, as though talking to himself, he said: 'It's not the kid — I never saw the kid, I can't feel anything about her. It's my wife. That kid was *everything* to her — God! she loved that kid. All her letters, all she talked about was the kid. All I want to do' — he clenched and opened his fist and looked at the fingers — 'is to be there for the funeral. If I could just get her through that, I think she'd be all right. I could make it, too, if I could get out of here tomorrow or Thursday.' He looked up quickly at the others.

'You'll get out,' Bergstrom said. 'This time tomorrow night you'll be on a plane.'

Thompson nodded impatiently, as though talking to a man of incomplete information. 'I'll get out,' he said flatly. 'If they won't do anything for me over there, I'm going over the hill. I've got it all figured out.'

'Now take it easy,' Braue said mildly.

'I'm not kidding,' said Thompson. Suddenly he picked up a ruler and flung it against the bulkhead; for a moment his eyes were frantic. Then he folded his hands and said quietly: 'I'm not kidding. If they won't do anything for me, I'll type myself up a set of orders and forge the Old Man's name. Then I'll stick some clothes

in a bag and go over there again Thursday and get on
a plane. I could be home before the Old Man knows
what hit him.'

Braue and Bergstrom glanced at each other. 'Take it
easy, Frank,' Braue said uncomfortably. 'You can't do
that.'

Thompson looked coolly at them. 'I'm not kidding,'
he said quietly.

Bergstrom, watching him closely, knew that this
wasn't just talk. He saw and measured his friend's desperate intensity, and felt it equal to almost anything.
He spun a paperweight on the desk. 'Well,' he said
finally, 'you won't have to do that. This time tomorrow
night you'll be on a plane. You wait and see.'

Thompson didn't say anything. After a while, because he had the four-to-eight again in the morning,
Bergstrom left the two still sitting in the yeoman's
office and went down and turned in. It was stifling hot
in the compartment, and he lay in his bunk a long time
and couldn't sleep. He smoked a cigarette and thought
of Thompson. He remembered the desperation he had
seen on Thompson's face. Goddamn, Bergstrom
thought, he's really taking it hard. He's really pounding his head against the wall. It was after midnight
when he finally got to sleep, and Thompson still wasn't
in his bunk.

When he was called at three-thirty, Bergstrom got up
and dressed beside the bunk. He looked into the top
bunk. Thompson was there, lying on his back, head
propped on a pillow, wide staring awake.

'Take it easy,' Bergstrom whispered.

'I'm all right,' Thompson answered. 'I'm just going to San Diego, that's all.'

'Naw, take it easy,' Bergstrom said. 'I'll see you to-night.' He went up to take the watch. At eight o'clock, when he came off, Thompson had already gone ashore. It was a long ride over to the big island, and Bergstrom knew the boat would be late getting back. It was three-thirty in the afternoon, almost time to take the watch again, when Thompson returned.

Bergstrom was digging in his locker for cigarettes when Thompson came down to the compartment. 'Whew!' said Thompson, and flopped wearily across Bergstrom's bunk. His dungarees were salt-streaked where they had dried from wetting, his face and arms were sunburned pink, and his eyes were red with the sun and with fatigue. After a moment he pulled himself up and sat on the edge of the bunk, and with infinite slowness untied his shoelaces. Then he kicked off his shoes and grinned suddenly at Bergstrom. 'Wow!' he said, 'what a day!' Still smiling curiously, he shook his head. 'Two hours over, and two hours back, and taking seas both ways. And walk, Jesus, did I walk!' With the same patient weariness he started to unbutton his shirt.

Bergstrom watched him. 'How did you make out?' he asked.

Thompson stretched and pulled off his shirt. 'No soap,' he said. 'I went to the Chaplain and I went to the flag secretary and they both told me the same thing: if the Captain wouldn't approve it, I couldn't get any emergency leave. They said it was all up to the Captain. So' — he was examining the sunburn on his arms — 'I went over to the Red Cross and they got off a telegram for me.'

'Nothing doing, eh?' said Bergstrom. 'That's too bad. I thought they could probably do something for you.'

Thompson got up and peeled off his trousers. He shook his head. 'Couldn't do a thing. I really felt lousy when they told me that; I really felt bad. I had about three hours before the boat shoved off and so I just started walking. I walked for three hours, up one road and down another, way up past some Seabee camp, and up a little mountain and down along the beach — I didn't give a damn where I was going. I just had to walk — I really felt mean. I got so far away I had to run the last mile to catch the boat. I must have walked at least twenty miles all together, but I felt better when I got through. I felt a hell of a lot better.' He stood in his shorts and the sudden, curious grin came back to his face. 'Jesus,' he said, 'that's more walking than I've done in four years. I'll be stiff as a board tomorrow.'

Bergstrom was about to say again that he was sorry they couldn't do anything, but Thompson seemed already to have forgotten it. So he said: 'I'll see you at eight,' and went up for the watch. He was glad to see that Thompson was taking it all right. He was glad to see that he wasn't talking and acting and feeling like he did last night. He'd be all right now, Bergstrom figured. Probably be down in the dumps for quite a while yet, but he'd get over that. He'd have plenty of time to get over that. The thing to do was to talk with him and keep his mind occupied so that he wouldn't brood.

That was Bergstrom's purpose when he came off watch again at eight: he thought he'd find Thompson and get him off with Braue somewhere for a bull session. When he went through the messhall, he found Thompson all right. The Monopoly session was going full blast and Thompson was right in the middle of it. The game was noisier than Bergstrom ever remembered it, and Thompson seemed to be having a wonderful time. Some particularly choice piece of crookedness had just been pulled off and Thompson was laughing so hard that the tears came to his eyes. And, while Bergstrom watched, Thompson's hand fell casually to the table and filched a pile of money from the man beside him. The other kibitzers noticed, too, and shouted noisy approval, and Thompson went off again into peals of laughter. He seemed just about the happiest man in the world.

Watching this scene, Bergstrom was suddenly and sharply disturbed. He stayed a moment longer, then he left the messhall and went up to the yeoman's office. His friend Braue was alone in there, writing a letter. Bergstrom shut the door and sat down.

'Have you seen Thompson since he got back?' he began.

Braue scrawled a few more lines on his letter and sealed the envelope. 'Yeah,' he said. 'He didn't do any good over there. They told him it was all up to the Captain.'

Bergstrom nodded. His brow wrinkled in a frown. 'You know how he was talking last night?'

Braue leaned back in his chair and nodded.

'You know how crazy he was last night? Ready to go over the hill and everything? Really pounding his head against the wall?'

Braue nodded.

Bergstrom went on: 'Really broken up about it, really taking it hard?'

'What about it?' Braue asked.

'Well,' said Bergstrom, 'tonight he's sitting down in the messhall playing Monopoly as though there wasn't a thing in the world had happened. Having the time of his life.'

Braue picked up a pencil and studied it minutely.

'How about that?' Bergstrom asked puzzledly. 'Last night he was batting his head against the wall. Tonight he's right back in the old groove. What about that: is that right?'

Braue didn't answer right away. He was a quiet and thoughtful boy, highly regarded on the ship. He twisted the pencil around in his hand and squinted as though he were examining a diamond. 'Well,' he said finally, 'if you really want to get technical, what the hell can he do?'

Bergstrom thought that over for a moment, and then he had to admit it was right: what in the hell could he do?

It was about ten in the morning when Stoltz, the radioman, went around and awakened Mr. Billings, the communication officer. There was a message to the ship for Mr. Billings to break. Billings mumbled and groaned and finally got up. This was an occupational hazard: about once a month the ship would receive a message and he would have to get out of bed to break it. He always did get up, though, because he always got excited at the possibility that the message might be his orders.

He got excited now, and when he went up to the radio shack and saw that the message was from the Bureau he got more excited. Feverishly he started breaking it and got as far as 'Lieut.' . . . Then he stopped to catch his breath. If the next group was 'jg' it might be his orders. He went on. The next word was Douglas, and the orders were for Roberts. Back to the States for reassignment.

After his first disappointment had passed, Billings decided he was very glad for Roberts. If any officer deserved orders, it was Roberts. Billings typed up the message and ran down to show it to him. He found Roberts at number two hatch, watching while some dunnage was removed from the bottom. 'Your orders!' Billings shouted, and showed him the message.

Roberts read it, and then looked up and studied Billings: 'Are you kidding?' he said flatly.

'No, I ain't kidding,' Billings said. 'This is on the level, Doug!'

Roberts studied him for a moment longer, then he read the orders again; and then all of a sudden he grinned. He just stood and grinned the widest and most foolish grin Billings had ever seen. He must have stood like that for at least three minutes, not saying a word. Then suddenly, still grinning, he grabbed Billings's

overseas cap and flung it over the side. He pounded
Billings on the back and started pushing him toward
the house. 'Come on!' he said. 'I'll buy you a cup of
coffee!'

You had to give the Captain credit, he was unpredictable. As Roberts explained to Billings, he fully expected the old bastard to hold him a month or two,
just out of spite, before detaching him. Although the
orders read that he was to be *immediately* detached,
Roberts had cause to know that the Old Man was not
impressed by Bureau directives. The orders of the last
officer to get off, Ensign Soucek, had read the same
way; and the Captain had kept him for a full month.
Roberts expected at least equal treatment.

But the Captain fooled him. Fooled him wonderfully. When Billings finally took him the message, he
read it and sniffed and grunted. He delivered to
Billings a brief, ordinary harangue on the subject of
Roberts. Then he said with sudden decisiveness: 'All
right, that's fine! We'll get rid of that guy fast. You
tell the executive officer to write up his orders and get
him off of here tomorrow. Yessir, by God, we'll get
rid of that guy in a hurry!' Then the Captain smiled
his most gloating, cat-swallows-the-mouse smile. He
didn't know it, but he could scarcely have done anything nicer for Roberts if he had wanted to: which certainly he didn't.

It was a wonderful day for Roberts. Everything followed with miraculous precision. Billings had been over
on the beach the day before, and coming back he had

given a ride to an armed guard officer from a merchant
tanker. The officer had mentioned that his ship was
sailing straight to San Francisco day after tomorrow.
Billings, remarkably, even remembered the name of the
ship and with Roberts's enthusiastic consent, and without consulting the Captain, he had this message sig-
naled over: 'Can you take one officer passenger back to
the States?' In a very few minutes the answer came
back: 'Affirmative. Have him aboard by noon tomorrow.' Straight to the States on a fast merchant ship, the
most comfortable transportation possible. It was a wonderful day for Roberts. Before he could change his
mind, the Captain signed the orders detaching him, and
Mr. LeSueur, the executive officer, promised him a
boat any time in the morning that he wanted it.

Roberts spent the afternoon packing. By virtue of the
circumstances that normally odious process became a
very happy one. Roberts had a fine time throwing the
accumulated non-essentials and undesirables of two-
and-a-half-years' living into a mounting pile in the
corner. He was aided by — or at any rate he had for
company — Ensign Pulver. Pulver was considerably
depressed by the news, and he lay in Roberts's bunk,
propped on one elbow, and made lugubrious conversation. Finally the combination of a soft bunk and a
horizontal position proved too much and he fell asleep.
By dinnertime Roberts was all packed, and the pile in
the corner was mountainous.

Dinner that evening was quite an exciting meal for
all the officers. It was a genuine event when any officer

got orders, but when that officer was Roberts it was really so. It was a noisy dinner. Every officer in the wardroom shouted bawdy admonitions at Roberts. If he was asked once, he was asked twenty times: 'What's going to be the second thing you do when you hit Frisco?' Then Jake Bailey, the steward, brought out a big chocolate cake. He had laboriously lettered in white frosting, 'So long, Mr. Roberts.' He was grinning sadly as he brought it over for Roberts to cut.

After dinner the Doc came over and said offhandedly to Roberts: 'Drop around after while.' It was the Doc's way of announcing that alcohol would be available in his room that night.

It took Roberts a couple of hours to turn over to Carney, his successor, all the records and Title B cards of the First Lieutenant. It was eight o'clock before he got around to the Doc's room. The door was closed and Pulver and Ed Pauley were already there. Ensign Pulver was lying in the Doc's bunk with a drink balanced on his stomach. The Doc poured a half-inch of grain alcohol in a water glass, filled it halfway from a can of orange juice, and handed the drink to Roberts. 'Sit down,' he said.

This was not the first time that the four had gathered there, and it was not the thirty-first. In a period of one year this group had consumed an impressive portion of the Doctor's supply of medicinal grain alcohol. Mixed with any type of fruit juice available in the pantry, it made a nice drink. Indeed, as the Doc was fond of saying, this war would likely produce a whole generation of alcohol and fruit-juice drinkers. These sessions in the Doc's room were always pleasant. The Doc always presided and he did most of the talking; but that was all right because the Doc was a wonderful talker and he had wonderful stories to tell. The rôles of Roberts and Ed Pauley were those of appreciative listeners and contributing philosophers. Ensign Pulver performed adequately as the foil.

These social nights passed easily in thoughtful talk. Sex was perhaps the favorite and certainly the inevitable subject. Ship's gossip and personalities, notably the Captain, were another. The great parent organization, the Navy, was frequently examined. These were the staples, but derivative or even extraneous subjects were permitted. Specialties were indulged, and Roberts and the Doc held long private discussions of medical matters. Ed Pauley, a fine, droll story-teller, spun an oral saga of life in Oswego, New York. When the conversation had not to do with sex, Ensign Pulver didn't contribute much.

The evening started out according to plan. At first there was polite discussion of Roberts's orders. There was speculation as to how much time in the States he would get, and after that, what type of duty he would draw. It was mentioned that he was lucky to get a ride straight back to Frisco. Then, very skillfully, Ed Pauley transferred the talk to sex. The transition was smooth.

'Doug,' he said to Roberts, 'do you rape easily? Because from what I read about the States, you'll probably be attacked in the middle of Market Street by one of those predatory American women.'

This provoked a long and thoughtful discussion of the mores and morals of American womanhood. All in all, it consumed a period of three drinks. It was ground that had been covered before, but on which the definitive word had not yet been said. The talk was almost scholarly. Regional differences in the sexual habits and aptitudes of women were carefully probed. Ed Pauley did an exhaustive job on the propensities of the girls of Oswego. Ensign Pulver was listened to with the respect due an authority as he offered for contrast the reproductive rhythm of Scranton, Pennsylvania. Lieutenant Roberts spoke briefly but searchingly of the peculiarities of the Middle West in general, and Chicago in particular. When all the evidence was in, it remained for the Doc to attempt the definitive word.

'We are embarking,' he hypothesized, 'on a new and revolutionary era in the history of sex. In quite a literal sense, women during this war have discovered sex and they have found it a field of human activity which they can dominate. From the traditional rôle of passivity in sexual relations, they have passed beyond partnership into aggressiveness. From now on, women will be the aggressors in the sex act. Sometime early next year, and probably in San Francisco, we will read of the first criminal assault of a boy by a girl. Soon after that, the matter will become so commonplace it will not be newsworthy. All the assertive functions of courting will be usurped by women; they will send flowers, buy

candy, pay for dinners, and in general initiate and control reproduction in all its manifestations. It is probably,' the Doc concluded, 'some sort of a millennium.'

There was a moment of respectful silence when the
Doc finished. Then, because they were all thirsty after
the intense discipline of the seminar, the Doctor poured
more drinks. The talk relaxed into loose and anecdotal
discussion. Ed Pauley mentioned his friend who had
rendered the same girl pregnant six times within the
space of thirteen months. Pauley offered it as some sort
of a record, and the Doc agreed that it very likely was.
The Doctor brought up the well-known movie actress
whom he had treated for alcoholic nyphomania. Then
one of the rituals of their gatherings was acted out.
While Ensign Pulver lay in the bunk and grinned
hugely, the purity of his fiancée back in Scranton, Pennsylvania, was systematically impugned. Ensign Pulver
always enjoyed this part of the evening immensely. He
alternately grinned and chuckled while all the probabilities were invoked. Tonight Lieutenant Roberts introduced a new twist when he suggested that Pulver
could send his girl no nicer nor more appropriate
Christmas gift than a chastity belt. He further suggested that the carpenter shop could make a very fine
one. Pauley and the Doc concurred heartily, and
Ensign Pulver rolled on the bed in delighted laughter.

If Dowdy had not appeared, the evening would perhaps have gone on like that, deep in its routine, and
ended in comparative tranquility. If Dowdy had not
appeared, perhaps the Doctor would have remained

merely pensively philosophical. Perhaps: although these things are by no means certain. It could be persuasively argued that the imminent departure of Lieutenant Roberts was too shocking a mutation for the ship to absorb without a brief, compensatory period of chaos. Or it could be more baldly argued that certain factions of the ship's company were simply ready for a good bender. At any rate, Dowdy did appear, and the evening did attain to a certain violence; and the Doctor did, to a certain extent, go berserk.

As a drunk the Doc was of the unpredictable sort. Up to a certain point he was disciplined if loquacious. Beyond that point the Doc got pretty primitive. There was the time at an officers' club at one of the islands when he tried to do battle with a four-striper. 'Silly-looking, pot-bellied oaf,' he had called the four-striper, who was not only twice his rank but twice his size as well. If he had not been also twice as drunk, the Doctor would undoubtedly have been a candidate for Portsmouth Naval Prison. That was one time, and there had been several others.

It was after ten o'clock when Dowdy knocked on the door. He stood sober and purposeful in the doorway. 'Hear you're leaving us?' he addressed Roberts. When this was confirmed, he went on: 'Well, a few of us are having a little party down in the armory and they said for me to ask you down to have a drink with us. That's all of you, naturally,' he added.

Roberts questioned the Doc with a look. 'Sure thing,' said the Doc expansively. 'Hell, yes, we'll have a drink. But first you have one with us.'

Dowdy did that, and he did better than that: he had two. Then the Doc said: 'We might as well take this with us.' He picked up the quart of alcohol, now reduced to less than a pint, stuck it under his shirt, and then, in single file, the Doc leading, Ensign Pulver trailing, the group repaired to the armory.

They met a noisy reception. The new party was already in an advanced state. The armory was not a large room and now it was crowded. There was Olson, of course, and there was Stefanowski, of course. Kalinka, the shipfitter, and Vanessi, the storekeeper, were sitting on the workbench. The two gunner's mates, Wiley and Schaffer, were leaning on the rifle rack. Denowsky was not fixed but mobile, wandering up and down. The large ten-gallon crock sat on the deck in almost the geometrical center of the room.

Right away the Doc made a perfect gesture, one that symbolically and in fact wedded the two groups. He pulled out the bottle of alcohol, flourished it and emptied its contents into the crock. The cheers were almost deafening.

Dowdy was equal to his duties as host and he poured drinks of the amalgamated alcohol and jungle juice for the newcomers. 'This here is a brand-new batch,' he explained to them. 'It turned out pretty good. The last batch we made, there was something the matter with it. I guess we let it set too long — it had kind of a green crust on top. Wiley there drank some and he peed green the next day. What do you suppose caused that, Doc?'

'Oh, some kind of a fungus growth in the bladder,' the Doc said airily. 'This is good stuff.'

'Yeah,' said Dowdy. 'Anyway, I give that last batch away to the engineers. It didn't look good to me, and you can't hurt an engineer.'

Then the toasts began. Stefanowski made the first, and, considering the occasion, it was just about perfect. Although he stood a little unsteadily, his words were firm and brave: 'Now, by God, this drink is for the best damn officer I know, and that's Mister Roberts. And that ain't saying nothing against the rest of you officers because I think we got a good bunch of officers on this ship —' Stefanowski paused and qualified: 'Except for that shithead of a Captain — and I think we got the best of the lot here tonight. But, by God, I say, and I bet you other officers agree with me, that Mister Roberts is absolutely the tops, and I'm sure sorry to see him go, and, by God, I think we ought to drink to him!' It is hard to see how it could have been more nicely put, and Stefanowski's toast was promptly and noisily executed.

There were many others. The toast idea caught the fancy of the party, and the level of the improved jungle juice went down markedly in the crock. After all present had been honored, toasts were drunk to, among others: Bela Kun, Chili Williams, the Captain's early demise, Girls Who Wore Black Pants, Girls Who Wore Pink Pants, Girls Who Wore No Pants, Cordell Hull, Winnie Ruth Judd, Boo-Boo Hoff, and Marjorie Ann Lundberg, of Coffeyville, Kansas. These necessarily took a long time, though not as long as you might expect, and in the course of them Dowdy sidled over to Lieutenant Roberts.

'Say,' he said secretively, 'Tom Olson's got a good idea. He says we ought to take care of the Old Man's palm trees tonight. You know the Old Man's got that watch up there now, but Olson says that Red McLaughlin went on at midnight, and hell, if he did, he's asleep by now. Hell, it's twelve-fifteen, and you know Red McLaughlin. So maybe if you and me and Olson sort of sneak up there now . . .'

The thing was done with style. Dowdy was right: Red McLaughlin was asleep, propped against the Captain's bulkhead. The two palm trees were removed from their five-gallon cans and dumped over the side. Red McLaughlin was sleeping with both arms outstretched and the empty cans were thoughtfully placed within their compass. Dowdy and Olson did everything — they insisted it was their turn. Roberts's rôle was that of honored observer, and when they finished, he complimented the boys on a thoroughly professional job.

The evening should have ended there. Right then and there it was a success. It had form, and accomplishment, and a nice feeling. Unfortunately the others in the armory had not this sense of structure and of proportion. Dowdy and Olson and Lieutenant Roberts weren't absent very long on their mission, but when they returned to the party, they found it noticeably deteriorated.

A bitter argument was going on. Denowsky stood accused of urinating in the crock of jungle juice. Everyone was standing around the crock and Schaffer was holding Wiley, who was making spasmodic attempts to swing at Denowsky. Everyone was shouting. It was a bad moment, and the Doctor's intervention was well-timed. 'Quiet!' he yelled until he finally got it. Then, very pompously, he announced that he would make a test. While all watched, he took two glasses. He dipped one into the jungle juice and filled it. Then he looked around and on the workbench he spotted a bottle of ink. He emptied this into the other glass. He held the two glasses up and alternately poured one into the other, as though preparing a bromo-seltzer. Then, in his best scientific manner, one eye screwed shut and his face impartial, he held the glasses up to the light. He had almost breathless attention as he studied them. Finally he put down the glasses and made a gesture like a baseball umpire signaling a runner safe. 'It's okay,' he announced authoritatively; 'the test is negative.'

The decision was greeted with cheers; the acquitted man Denowsky was pounded on the back, and Wiley, released from restraint, promptly made another lunge at him. Finally Wiley was placated and the party resumed. It grew in size and in volume. It was depleted by one when Vanessi passed out quietly and was removed to the passageway, but then it soon acquired Dolan, the quartermaster, and Morris, the signalman, and Ringgold, and two other first division men.

It was no longer possible to move from one end of the armory to the other. The party divided into several autonomous groups. One, with Wiley and Schaffer, sat on the deck in a corner and sang a new set of lyrics to 'On, Wisconsin.' The new lyrics consisted solely of a popular and colloquial four-letter verb or noun chanted over and over. Kalinka was the center of the little group in the opposite corner. Kalinka had been demonstrating the process of placing one's leg behind one's head; now his leg was locked behind his head and he couldn't get it down. It didn't seem to bother him, though; and in truth he didn't seem aware of it. He just sat on the deck and talked with a drink in his hand. A third group gathered around the Doctor and tried to convince him that they were deserving cases for medical discharge.

It was about this time the Doc decided that the punch was getting flat. He said it needed more alcohol and he said he knew where there was some if Olson could get him a hack-saw. Olson managed that right away, and the Doc said, 'Come on!' Wiley went along and very furtively the three went to the medical storeroom and with much sweating effort sawed away the hinge of the lock. With a high sense of achievement they removed another quart. The Doc had the keys in his pocket, but he had evidently forgotten this. Only an equal forgetfulness on the part of the other two, or a rare sense of honor, saved the vulnerable alcohol locker from further and serious depletion that night.

Ringgold was the first casualty. Stefanowski had invented a game which became instantaneously popular. He would pour benzine on a trash-can full of oily rags, ignite the can, and step back while everyone else ran to the washbasin and drew water and threw it on the fire. They would fill whatever was at hand — glasses, helmets, a Silex bowl — and they would throw the water in the general direction of the fire while shouting such things as, 'Here comes old Hook and Ladder Number Three!' Pretty soon there was an inch of water on the deck. Stefanowski built some splendid soaring fires, and the game would probably have gone on for a long time if Ringgold hadn't been hit in the back of the neck by a heave of scalding water.

Stefanowski's game converted him to a full-fledged pyromaniac. When a little later, Dowdy started forward to the head, he followed down the passageway a trail of three blazing trash-baskets. He located Stefanowski in the compartment, sitting on the deck beside his bunk, busily soaking his pillow with benzine. Dowdy raised Stefanowski's head to sufficient height, and held it in position with one hand while the other landed a sturdy uppercut. He placed Stefanowski in his bunk and went away with the bottle of benzine.

It was about two o'clock when it came to Ensign Pulver that he could walk on water. He announced his discovery to the party, and some believed him and some didn't. It was decided that he should demonstrate. The whole party, less Kalinka and Morris, who stayed with him, surged up to the quarterdeck. They stood at the rail while Pulver walked down to the foot of the gangway and stepped off as casually as from a curb. There was a strong current running, and although Pulver threshed energetically he was slipping rapidly astern. Denowsky decided that Pulver was drowning, and he climbed over the rail and jumped twenty feet into the water to save him. Both of them would probably have been swept out to sea if Stevens, the gangway watch, had not also been a qualified coxswain and an alert boy. Stevens scurried down the jacob's-ladder into the LCVP tied alongside, started it up and went after the two. He had quite a time rounding them up. Although Pulver lay sprawled across the stern sheets, Denowsky for a long time insisted that he had drowned and wouldn't get out of the water.

When the two swimmers were finally laid out on the quarterdeck, Lieutenant Roberts left the party. He left it in heated discussion as to whether artificial respiration should be applied to Pulver and Denowsky, who lay on their backs and participated in the debate. Roberts slipped up the ladder and made it safely to his room. Although he was far from sober, he did two very wise and practical things: he locked the door and he set his alarm clock for six-thirty.

The wisdom of the first was demonstrated a few minutes later when there came loud voices and vigorous pounding on his door. Roberts kept quiet and finally the visitors went away.

He had set the early alarm because, although he was not at his most acute, it was clear to him that there would be unpleasant repercussions from the party.

Roberts thought it entirely possible that the Captain might seek to identify him with the night's doings, and might further seek to detain him for a few days or a few months. Roberts was going to get away before the Captain got up.

The wisdom of this decision was emphasized not so very much later. Roberts had just fallen asleep when he was awakened by a crashing noise. At the time, he thought it the report of a five-inch gun, although he supposed it could be a bomb. He was not disposed to be curious, and he went back to sleep; very grateful that he was in bed with the door locked.

At six-thirty the clatter of the alarm was horrible. Roberts heard it and awoke, and it seemed to him inconceivable that he could ever move again. His head was one great pounding agony and his stomach was so raw he thought it exposed. But as he lay in bed he recalled what was at stake; and finally, slowly, and with an awful dragging care, he got up. Slowly he dressed and slowly he walked down to the wardroom. There he drank a glass of orange juice and asked Jackson, the steward's mate, to bring down his gear. He took paper and scribbled little notes to Pulver and the Doc and Ed Pauley and Mr. LeSueur. It was seven-fifteen when he went out to the officer-of-the-deck to request a boat.

Ensign Moulton had the deck and he clarified the matter of the explosion. It seemed that the party, at the Doc's suggestion, had decided to hold loading drill on the five-inch gun. There were dummy shells back there, and the drill had gone along uneventfully until some loader with a passion for realism introduced a live shell from the ready box. Some other realist pulled the lanyard on the firing pin. The shell had grazed the top of the mast of a ship half a mile astern and had dropped, it was hoped, safely out to sea. Moulton added that there would probably be all kinds of hell raised by the Captain and by the island commander.

Roberts thought so, too, and he was glad when the boat came around. He shook hands with Moulton, asked him to say good-bye to everyone, and got aboard. It was a fifteen-minute boat ride over to the tanker, and all the way Roberts sat in the stern sheets with his head in his hands and tried desperately not to be sick. It occurred to him that he should feel some emotion at leaving the *Reluctant*, but beyond his own physical misery there wasn't a thing. He didn't even look back. When he got to the tanker and stood at the head of the gangway, he did turn around to look for the ship which had been his existence and his despair for two and a half years. But in the forest of distant masts he couldn't even be certain which one it was.

THERE IS A PHRASE, 'magnetic personality,' which, through the blurring and misuse common to our language, has come to designate any person sufficiently noisy at a party to compel attention. Even used with discipline, the term is inadequate, but still and all, it is valid. There are people of wonderful conductivity who draw rather than repel the tenuous and tentative approaches that we call human relationships, and through whom, as through a nerve center, run the freely extended threads of many lives. The plotted lives of most of us would show as lonely, atomic dots connected by a few wavering and accidental lines; while people of this special quality would emerge as the exact and inevitable intersection of a whole complex of sighted lines. The quality that they possess is not an aggressive one, not a conscious one, and it can never be one acquired. It is native and inescapable and may even be unwelcome to its inheritor. It admits of greater loneliness than is commonly thought possible. It is completely inaccessible to analysis, and about all you can say of its composition is that perhaps it has to do with 'life force,' a concept equally nebulous. This quality of attraction and cohesiveness is, like most ineffables, best observed in its own void: when its possessor leaves a group of which he was a unit, he invariably depletes it by much more than one unit. Often his absence will mean the dissolution of the group.

Lieutenant Roberts was that sort of person, and dissolution is what happened when he left the *Reluctant*. In a very real sense, he had held the ship together. Awakening to the prospect of each toneless and reiterated day, every man on the ship took some degree of sustenance from the simple awareness that Roberts was aboard. Even the engineers, who hadn't cause to know him, would invent oblique ways to talk with him. In a curious way he ministered to and filled a great collective lack. Perhaps it was that an intensity sufficient for the allotted threescore years and ten was compressed into his short life. At any rate, he had that power. He was friendly, but not aggressively so, and he worked hard and was often tired, and when he was tired he could be very sharp and sarcastic. He had a desperate humor, and he had great tolerance and, probably, much humility. The crew members imposed on him outrageously with their demands for his talk, his time, his counsel. He held the ship together as a magnet holds filings, and when he left, the filings fell into clustered and undirected confusion.

Everything seemed to go wrong. Lieutenant Carney took over the job of First Lieutenant, and everything went wrong out on deck. Carney proved to be flagrantly incompetent, and under his direction the loading or unloading took hours and sometimes days longer than it should. There was a lot of bitterness about that. The ship got some bad water at one of the islands, and there was an epidemic of diarrhea. Martin, a second division man, fell from the second deck level to the bottom of number three hatch, fracturing his pelvis and breaking both legs. Everyone was in an ugly humor. The Captain ordered that any man caught in his bunk after reveille go on report. Furthermore, he saw to it that Mr. LeSueur, the executive officer, enforced the order. The first morning nine-tenths of the crew were on report. Mr. LeSueur himself became nasty and treacherous. There were any number of quarrels and fights. There was an almost daily fist-fight, and once Cornwall, the Captain's boy, took a knife to Jake Bailey, the chief steward, and cut him up severely about the arms.

The ship's disspirit was so extreme that nobody bothered, or thought to bother, the Captain's palm trees. There were now four of them replacing the two that disappeared the night of Roberts's going-away party. The Captain had decided that Roberts was solely responsible for the palm-tree business, and after a while he secured the watch on the wing of the boat deck. He got very apoplectic whenever he talked about Roberts, and for two weeks he coarsely assured everyone available that he would tear Roberts apart if he ever saw him again. Meanwhile, the four little palm trees in their five-gallon Foamite containers stood in a neat, unguarded row on the wing, and nobody thought to touch them.

But the biggest change of all was in Ensign Pulver. From a remarkably genial young man he became overnight a remarkably disagreeable one. He had been slow and almost unknown to wrath. Now, he was in his best mood merely surly, and in his worst, which predominated, he was downright belligerent. He was insufferable. He picked quarrels with the other officers over trifles. He shouted at and abused the steward's mates. One night at dinner he almost came to blows with Ed Pauley over the issue of a napkin. After that he wasn't on speaking terms with Pauley. He wasn't, in fact, on speaking terms with most of the other officers. The Doc was about the only one who would have anything to do with him these days. He gave up his reading program altogether and took to sitting moodily in his room and playing endlessly on the harmonica, over and over, the only tunes that he knew: 'Row the Boat Lightly' and 'Flow Gently, Sweet Afton.' He drove everyone in officers' country nearly to distraction. And he took to roving the ship restlessly late at night, and to sitting up all hours in a folding chair on the quarterdeck. He was very lost.

He heard twice from Roberts after he left the ship. After the farewell party, Pulver wrote ahead to Roberts's home in Chicago. In that letter he told Roberts how the Captain blamed him for the second sabotage of his trees, and he reproduced as well as he could the texture of the Captain's threats against Roberts. He told Roberts of the *four* palm trees. Roberts wrote back about three weeks later. He said that the palm trees should certainly be dumped as a scientific experiment to determine whether they squared in number each time, or merely doubled. Roberts was at home then on a twenty-five-day leave. He said he'd write again when he got his new orders.

Ensign Pulver received Roberts's second letter on the same day that he got the news of his death. That was on August first, a few days before the first atomic bomb was dropped, a few weeks from the end of the war. The *Reluctant* had been under way for a week, and it was late in the afternoon when she finally anchored in Ennui Bay. Steuben, the yeoman and mail clerk, was sent over to pick up the mail. There was quite a bit of mail, and it wasn't until after the movies, almost nine o'clock, that he got it all distributed.

Ensign Pulver got four letters. He took them to his room, lay down in his bunk, and opened them in the order in which they lay. The first was from his mother, who advised him to stay away from Japan. The second was from a girl in San Francisco whom he had known carnally, and with whom he was trying to maintain friendly relations against his possible return to the States. The tone of her letter assured him that prospects were still good. The third letter was from Lieutenant Roberts. The date-mark was three weeks old. It said that he was now on a destroyer, and that he'd been flown out all the way from the States to catch it. He was replacement for the First Lieutenant, who had gone off his nut and had been transferred to a hospital ship. Roberts sounded very pleased with the duty, and mentioned that there was on board a fellow named Fornell who had gone through the University of Alabama with Pulver. Roberts wrote: 'Fornell says that you and he used to load up your car with liquor in Birmingham and then sell it at indecent profit to the fraternity boys at Alabama. How about that?' Pulver smiled happily when he read that. So Roberts and Fornell were on the same ship!

The last letter was from Fornell. It said that the can was now on its way to Pearl after taking a Kamikaze while running up and down off Kyushu. It said that the plane had gotten in just after they had secured from a four-hour G.Q., in the course of which six planes had come around and two had been shot down. This suicide must have been waiting very high, Fornell said, and it dropped straight down and hit on the port side of the bridge structure. It had killed everyone in a twin-forty battery and it had gone on through and killed Roberts and another officer drinking coffee in the wardroom. All told, four officers and seven men had been killed. Fornell added that Roberts hadn't been aboard three weeks, but that he seemed like one hell of a nice guy.

Ensign Pulver read the letter through to the end and then he folded it carefully into the envelope and placed it and the other letters in the space behind his mattress where he kept all of his mail. He had now the knowledge that Roberts was dead, but, as often happens, there was a lag between the fact and the implication, the wound and the pain. Pulver didn't feel much of anything. In his life, he had never had anything very unpleasant or extraordinary happen to him and now he didn't know quite what to do. He smoked a cigarette and finally decided that it was his responsibility to tell somebody.

He couldn't think right away whom to tell. A little curiously, he thought that it shouldn't be just anybody; it should be someone whom Roberts would want to know. It should be one of the people whom Roberts had liked best. They should know first, Pulver decided; the others could know in time. The Doctor, he must surely tell the Doctor; and Dowdy, Dowdy must know too. These two came immediately to Pulver's mind, and right now there weren't any others. He went to find the Doc.

But the Doc wasn't in his room and he wasn't in any of the other rooms. He must then be down in sick-bay, and Pulver didn't want to tell him there. He set out to find Dowdy. He went out on the quarterdeck and he found him right away. Lights had been rigged on the mast-table, and he could see Dowdy out on deck supervising removal of the hatch beams from number three. Pulver called to him. Dowdy nodded, and when the winch operator laid the beam safely on deck he came over.

Dowdy stood before him, passive and incurious. He had been working with wire cable, and he kept his leather gloves on.

Pulver said: 'Mister Roberts is dead. I just got the word in a letter.'

Dowdy didn't say anything. He looked up quickly and then he looked at him steadily. Pulver felt that every muscle of his face, every nerve and every pore, was under that gaze.

Pulver went on: 'He got orders to a can and the can got hit by a suicide plane off Japan. There were eleven of them killed altogether.' He didn't know anything else to say.

Dowdy held his gaze for a moment longer. Then, abruptly, he broke it off. 'Thanks,' he said. He turned then and walked away. Pulver saw that while he stood there Dowdy had removed his gloves.

He was beginning now to feel the pain. It was dull and desolate and smothering. He went back into the house and found the Doc. The Doc was undressing for a shower. He stepped out of his shorts and wrapped a towel about his waist as Pulver came in.

'Hi, Doc,' Pulver said. He leaned back wearily against the opened door.

'Hi,' said the Doc. He looked curiously at Pulver.

'Roberts is dead,' Pulver said in a flat voice. 'He was on a can and the can took a suicide plane off Japan.'

The Doc let out a soft whistle and sat down slowly on the edge of his desk. He studied Pulver with the same fixity as Dowdy.

'How did you find out?' he said finally.

'I got a letter from a guy I know who was on the same ship. A guy I used to know in college.'

The Doctor nodded slowly. He twisted his mustache and looked down at the deck.

Pulver spoke with sudden anguish: 'Isn't that rough, Doc? You know how he batted his head to get off of here? You know how he wanted to get in the war? And then, as soon as he gets out there, he gets killed.' His voice was almost pleading.

The Doc nodded and chewed his lip. 'That's funny,' he said thoughtfully.

'Funny?'

The Doc looked up. 'I don't mean funny, Frank,' he said softly. He paused for a moment. 'I mean that I think that's what he wanted.'

Ensign Pulver was startled. What did the Doc mean?

He was about to ask, but now the pain was getting bad, and suddenly he didn't want to talk any longer. He stood away from the door. 'Well,' he said vaguely, 'I just thought I'd tell you.'

The Doc didn't seem to hear right away. He was staring at the deck again. Then he said quietly: 'I'm glad you did.' And as Pulver started haltingly out the door, he called after him: 'I'm awfully sorry, Frank.'

Pulver turned around and nodded acknowledgment; then he went on down the passageway. He came to the wardroom and he thought of telling the people there. But the moment he looked in, he saw it was impossible. Carney and Billings were playing acey-deucy. Keith was sitting at one table writing letters, and Ed Pauley was drinking coffee. Moulton was over at the turntable playing records. It was all just the same. It was just as every night, days without end. Nothing had happened; and now Pulver saw that, in plain truth, nothing ever could happen to these men. The higher centers where action was absorbed, where thought impinged and desires spoke, had been determinedly shut off and allowed to atrophy, and all that remained was an irritable surface with an insatiable hunger for triviality. Apathy then was not a state of negation, but a faith of positiveness, and to practice it was to surrender to it. It had seemed to the men of this ship the only possible faith that could accommodate the facts of their existence, and at its demand they had reduced life to the monotone reflex that was only efficient, and, in the last analysis, the only possible, survival. Ensign Pulver had lived this life for over a year without objection and often with enjoyment. Now it seemed to him horrible. He winced that he had thought to tell these officers of Roberts's death and let them make of it a moment's diversion.

Abruptly he withdrew and plunged down the passageway. He went outside and walked along the rail of the house. On the starboard side, in the dark of the house, he found a place at the rail with no one about. He stood there a long time, staring at the dark plane of water, pierced here and there by shafts of yellow light. He studied the high, coldly remote red light atop the radio tower on the island. Roberts was dead. He felt a need to cry, and he looked around him furtively, and then, furtively, he tried it. Self-consciously, he whimpered aloud, but the sound was so strange to him that he stopped. Crying wouldn't help. Nothing would help, but suddenly, there was still something to do.

He went up the starboard ladder to the wing of the boat deck. He went over to the Captain's palm trees, standing in their neat, mute row, and one by one he picked them up, four of them, and threw them over the side. When he finished, he was panting more than could be accounted for by the exertion. He brushed his hands together carefully and went inside on the boat deck. A little detachedly he wondered: would there be eight of them out tomorrow, or sixteen?

The Captain was sitting, reading, in the large chair of his cabin. In the cone of harsh light from the floor lamp he looked old, and not evil, but merely foolish. He glanced up at the knock on the opened door.